THE ANALOGY OF EXPERIENCE

The
Analogy of Experience

AN APPROACH
TO UNDERSTANDING RELIGIOUS TRUTH

John E. Smith

Clark Professor of Philosophy
Yale University

HARPER & ROW, PUBLISHERS
New York, Evanston, San Francisco, London

FIRST EDITION

STANDARD BOOK NUMBER: 06-067420-2

LIBRARY OF CONGRESS CATALOG CARD NUMBER: 72-77820

Designed by Patricia G. Dunbar

For my mother and father

Contents

Preface

This book represents the Warfield Lectures for 1970, which I was invited to deliver at the Princeton Theological Seminary in February of that year. I wish to express my thanks to President James I. McCord and his colleagues both for the invitation and for the genial hospitality shown to me during my visit. I was particularly appreciative of the opportunity I had for conversations with a friend of long standing, Professor George Hendry. His sharpness of mind, his wit and his disarming candor make talking with him a delight. I want also to express gratitude to Professors Edward Dowey and Charles West for all their kindnesses, and to Professor George Thomas of Princeton University for the opportunity to continue discussions about the philosophy of religion first started many years ago.

The text represents the lectures substantially as delivered with the exception of Chapter III, which has been added for the purpose of further clarifying the central concept in the discussion.

I am much indebted to my wife, Marilyn, a member of the Department of Philosophy at Quinnipiac College, for many spirited discussions about the basic ideas and for helpful suggestions concerning style. Mrs. Alan Slatter conscientiously typed both the original lectures and the revised manuscript and I am happy to extend my appreciation for both tasks.

John E. Smith

New Haven
July 1972

Introduction

It is not likely that future historians will ever come to describe the mid-twentieth century as an age of faith. On the contrary, those who attend closely to the facts are well aware of the many forms in which it has been claimed that "God is dead," that religion is an anachronism, and that man is left alone in the cosmos. As the result of a series of upheavals—social, political, scientific, cultural —the world of the Western nations has seemed to outgrow its past and, almost overnight, to have acquired a paralyzing sense of the inadequacy of many of its hereditary institutions. Traditional patterns of thought and action no longer seem fitting, and from every side we encounter either a nihilism that smashes everything before it, or a frantic quest for new gods, new experiences, new bulwarks in the face of the loss not only of God but of man himself.

Religious institutions are finding themselves caught in the midst of these revolutions, and on a grand scale. The world itself as transformed by technology and our view of the world as reshaped in accordance with the scientific outlook have contributed much to the loss of the *sense* of God's reality. On the one hand, we seem to draw all of our strength from the secular dimension of life and the sense of dependence on any Power transcending ourselves begins to fade. On the other hand, there is no doubt that the dazzling successes exhibited by the sciences in their disclosure of the structures of things have made it very difficult to think of God in the traditional sense as one more reality standing in addition to the realities recognized in science. Our confusion in understanding how to conceive of God has prevented us from having that practical interest and concern for his reality which must accompany our acknowledgment of anything as "real." Even the most convinced believer must admit that there is much in the evil, the noise, the confusion, and the violence of modern life that makes it difficult for anyone to think of God as really being "there" in the sense in which he most assuredly thinks of himself as "being there." "As surely as I exist," we say, "I recall returning that book," but it is extremely doubtful that for most people at present the reality of God is as sure as that!

Moreover, the theological outlook expressive of the Christian faith seems to us strange in a revolutionary nuclear and lunar age; the language defining that outlook—sin, salvation, atonement, grace—has become opaque and, for those who are not theologians, these terms have either become meaningless or they are thought to describe what happens in some other and esoteric world that has no intelligible connection with the one in which we live. The classical language of theology seems wholly confined to the past; it is repeated in the modern world often in merely ceremonial fashion that is lacking in conviction.

If the modern world has lost God, man himself does not seem to be faring better. Not only is there a confusion of tongues concerning man and his nature, but for many modern thinkers there is no longer a distinctively human dimension to the cosmos: man is regarded as no more than a highly complex organism to be understood after the fashion of a psychological mechanism or a chemico-electronic system. And some of the desperate, anguished counterattempts to recover the reality of man by confronting him with freedom, life projects and unlimited responsibility for authenticity find that this recovery can be achieved only at the cost of denying God. Hence the formula that if God is, man is not; it seems that never before in the history of Western religion was there such alienation. Men struggled with and against God in former periods, but the absolute either/or with respect to the divine and human is an undeniably novel development.

I am not for the present joining the issues implicit in the many points at which the modern temper runs against the Christian tradition. Since we cannot successfully present the Christian position in the modern world without facing honestly the mind and the mood of our audience, it is essential that we understand the climate of opinion that prevails. Nor is this opinion confined to skepticism about the Christian conception of God, or to new conceptions of man without God; the modern search for meaningful existence has in addition led to the establishment of new and powerful secular substitutes for traditional Christianity involving surrogates for God, novel rituals, flights into the world of expanded consciousness, and even a new religion of esthetic feeling worshipping the thrill and emotional intensity of the moment together with the self-expression of the unique and, so it seems, inexhaustible individual. While these secular substitutes testify to the indelible religious roots of man's being, their very existence adds to the confusion of voices and makes more problematic the communication of the Christian ideas. For if, as Calvin declared, the human mind is like a continuously operating factory for the production of idols, the task of distinguishing legitimate from counterfeit coin will be extremely difficult.

Thus far I have concentrated largely on ideas in this brief sketch of the religious situation. Important and fundamental as these may be, there is another vast dimension of modern life that has to do with individual and social conduct, with political oppression, radical prejudice, war, and poverty. Christianity is more than a truth about life; it is a form of life, a way of life for persons and a set of norms governing the relations between man and man. The Gospel of John sums this up through the words of Jesus: "I am the way, the truth and the life." It is, however, precisely this involvement in man's historical existence that poses monstrous problems for the reception of the Christian position. For so many of the horrendous events of our century, the cruelty, injustice and man's demonstrated inhumanity to man, have taken place within the confines of Christian civilization. It is, of course, true that there is considerable uncertainty about the validity of calling a civilization "Christian." And it is also true that critics, including those who do not believe in the possibility of a religious civilization in any sense, are determined to call Western civilization "Christian" so that they can then condemn it. But these considerations apart, the fact remains that Christianity has been the dominant religion of Europe, of Britain, and of America for centuries and it is clear that the failures of both churches and church members cannot be concealed. "If a man say, 'I love God' and hateth his brother, he is a liar." Judged in accordance with these strong words of the writer of the First Epistle of John, much of Christendom stands condemned, and the evidence is there for all to see.

Despite the many problems posed for Christianity by the present world situation, one important truth can be learned from the numerous criticisms that have been leveled against religion in general and the Christian faith in particular. There is an increasing sense of dissatisfaction with abstractions, with ideas and doctrines commended for their antiquity and their faithfulness to the past rather than for their illumination of present and future experience. In short, there is need to do again what was done so well by such thinkers as Augustine, Luther, Calvin, Schleiermacher and, in our own country, by Jonathan Edwards; to connect the meaning of theological ideas with human experience and to show their bearing on the life of each individual. As I shall argue, only through an experiential medium can we hope to recover a sense of the reality expressed through the Christian ideas. Whatever difficulties may stand in the way of presenting the Christian standpoint, there is some hope to be derived from the temper of the time. For that temper is expressed in a concern for experience, for the actual suffering and undergoing that makes up our encounter with the world and each other. In short, there is a demand to know the connections between what we are to believe and who we are and what we are to do. Christianity is well suited to that temper because of its central emphasis on a God who becomes ingredient in the world and its history through the medium of a Person who recapitulates man's experience in the ultimate dimension.

Christianity has never been set forth in a vacuum. If we consider the history of theology from the early Fathers to Barth and Tillich, we cannot miss the fact that those theologians who made the decisive impact were those who knew how to make an everlasting Gospel speak to their age in an intelligible way. The history of theology has not been a series of bare repetitions of the classical Christian content, but rather, creative reinterpretations of that content in the light of new knowledge and fresh experience. The "Treasure," to be sure, persists, but the "earthen vessels" in which it is contained change, and they change because history is a real order of development and our knowledge advances. If, for example, we recite the Apostles' Creed and a person seeking understanding asks us to explain its meaning, we have not fulfilled our obligation if we merely recite the Creed again. Joseph could repeat his dream to himself in its details over and over without coming any closer to his goal. He sought for an interpretation, for some interpreter who could tell him what his dream *meant* in a language he could understand. And in fulfilling his office, the interpreter not only reflects through his own mind the mind of his time, but his interpretation falls short of its goal unless it is cast in a form that Joseph can understand. So it is with the venture of theology; in each historical period we have to attempt to say what the classical Christian content means, something which cannot be done *merely* by repeating the ancient words and phrases, whether of the Bible or of past theologians. And unless we are to encapsulate that content in the past, forgetting that we are men who live and move not in the fourth century, or the thirteenth, but in the twentieth century, we shall have to take account of the social, scientific and cultural revolutions that have shaped the situation within which and to which we are to speak.

As a religion which takes time and history seriously as a medium of divine disclosure, Christianity cannot remain consistent with itself and at the same time ignore the novelties which the historical process brings forth. The reason that theology has a history in the first instance stems from advancing knowledge and changing social, political, and cultural circumstances. Insofar as the classical Christian content is meant to apply to historical reality embracing man and the world, that content must be understood in the light of new knowledge about its object. Let us compare, for example, the situation of a Calvin or an Augustine with that of the twentieth-century theologian. Both Augustine

and Calvin set forth, each in his own way, the Christian understanding of man, but it is clear that while the latter had to interpret Christianity against the background of sixteenth-century humanism, Augustine, though well versed in the ancient doctrine of
man, could know nothing of such a conception as was dominant
in Calvin's time. The present-day theologian is in a quite different position again; he confronts a Marxian, a Freudian, a Dar-
winian and a Sartrean man, and while his work as a theologian
is by no means entirely determined by these images of man, he
cannot afford to ignore them; and he could not if he would
because they have determined the climate in which he thinks and,
to a certain extent, even his own cast of mind. In this regard,
theology is always *zeitgebunden* and it cannot be otherwise; as we
have come to learn from Hegel, only God could write the timeless
theology.

Nor can the theologian attempt to resolve his problem by the
claim that he is talking about man only in the theological or
religious context and therefore that what is known about man in
other contexts is not relevant. For if the religious truth is meant
to be about man in his actual historical existence, it must be
related to *all* that is known about man from extratheological
sources. Insofar as our knowledge of ourselves and even our
human self-consciousness itself are subject to change, every doctrine of man, theological or philosophical, must reflect those
changes. Augustine's interpretation of the Christian doctrine of
man could not, *per impossibile*, have been determined in any way
by his response to the Freudian conception of human nature. The
fact is that in not knowing of some truths and plausible hypotheses about man that are now available, Augustine's references to
man were references to a being whom he but imperfectly understood. The contemporary theologian finds himself in a more
complex version of the same predicament. It is not that, in comparison with Augustine, he has anything like a perfect knowledge
of man derived from secular study, but rather, that he knows *more*
about man from these studies than Augustine did—and it is part
of his task to discover the relation of his theological doctrine to
that increment.

Again, in the adventure of theology, the factor that makes it necessarily dialectical is found in the need for creative reinterpretation whereby the theologian attempts to discover the relevant connections between the Gospel he has received and the dynamically changing present which he confronts. Although, according to Christianity, the disclosure of God in Christ and the total view of God, man, and the world implied together form a *final* revelation, the interpretation of that revelation is never absolutely final, and for two reasons: first, our insight into the content taken all by itself is never perfect (who, for example, will claim to have a final and certain understanding of the relation between the justice of God and that of man expressed in the Parable of the Laborers in the Vineyard?), and, second, since knowledge develops and climates of opinion change, the Christian content is continually being reinterpreted against new backgrounds of thought and action. This continuing encounter provides an opportunity for the theologian to increase our knowledge of faith and to discover new implications of that faith for life in the world. We see some results at present in the exploration of the resources in Christian faith for responding both to the legitimate challenges of Marxism, depth psychology, secularization, and the entire ecumenical enterprise. At each step, creative interpretation is called for, and, like Augustine setting out to write *De trinitate,* we must work in humility, and in the hope that our thought has the illumination of what was known among Augustinians as the Uncreated Light.

The consequences of the creative and open-ended character of theological interpretation for the communication of the Christian standpoint are clear and momentous. Let us consider what is involved. One seeks primarily to express a truth about human existence in relation to God and the world. Much depends on the manner in which the speaker becomes related to those to whom he speaks; the connection is not irrelevant and it is not a perfunctory affair. An interpreter aiming at creating understanding cannot assume an arrogant stance and "proclaim to" the hearer; on the contrary, his task is to "converse with" him in the hope of leading him to see or to understand. The contrast between "proclaiming to" and "conversing with" is of the utmost importance. The confrontation of modern man with Christian faith cannot take the form of a dogmatic and nondialectical proclamation of a final truth to the world. The "proclaiming to" approach unaccompanied by either understanding or love serves only to produce the negative reaction that further alienates men from God and from their fellows. One of the most manifest sins of Protestantism has been its too sanguine trust in the proclamation of the word by fallible men. Even if one were to agree that the hearing and understanding of the word has a logical priority over all visual and visible experience, the fact remains that proclamation confronts only the mind of the hearer without penetrating to a total life pattern and to that experience which the appropriation of a religious truth demands. The aim should be, rather, to engage the hearer, to "converse with" him in the hope of creating the possibility of his seeing what the interpreter believes he has seen.

The aim is not merely to "tell" another a truth as when we supply factual information in response to a question, but to lead another to see, to understand, to apprehend the truth for himself. Only in this way is it possible to pass beyond what Cardinal Newman called merely "notional assent." Wherever else Kierkegaard may have been correct in his interpretation of Christianity, he performed a distinct *dis*service in his critique of the Socratic method for leading anyone to understand anything. Neither Socrates nor the Socratic teacher is the Savior, but then no interpreter of the Christian view is the Savior either; the most one, as an interpreter, can hope to do is to present religious ideas in a way that helps others to see in Socratic fashion. Each, in the end, has to appropriate the truth for himself, and this cannot happen merely by being *told* this truth by another even in an ironic way. The parabolic speech of Jesus in his many conversations with disciples and others[1] illustrates the point quite clearly; the reli-

---

1. It is important to notice that Jesus did not always preach in the sense of "proclaim"; many of his most significant sayings result from *conversations* with quite ordinary people where he depends on them to grasp his point.

gious and theological point of a similitude is suspended, as it were, above the hearer and it is his task to see that point and appropriate it in his own situation. So with the Socratic dialectic; through conversing with another, one hopes to bring that person to see what he is driving at.

If Christianity is not to become a relic of the past, renewed attempts must be made to present it in an intelligible form. Modern man cannot be expected to take seriously an outlook that is merely archaic or totally lacking in connections with contemporary experience. I hope to explain in the succeeding chapters how this may be done. The task is that of synthesizing old and new. One sets out from a content stemming from the past. The next step is to attempt to understand that content and, through that understanding, to manifest the intelligibility implicit in the entire position. I shall begin by recalling the classical meaning of that ancient formula derived from the Septuagint version of Isaiah 7:9 —"faith seeking understanding." Next I shall set forth a new approach to understanding in the form of what I shall call the *analogia experientiae,* or the analogy of experience, aimed at showing how the structure of experience itself can function as the medium through which the religious perspective can be understood. With this foundation laid, I want to show how we might come to understand man as the being caught in a circular predicament, God as the transcending center of intention, Christ as the concrete manifestation of that center, and, finally, the church as the Beloved Community or locus of transforming power in the world.

In what follows, no attempt whatsoever will be made to "prove" that some theological doctrine or a given interpretation of such a doctrine must be accepted on pain of contradiction or illogicality. On the contrary, religion has never lived from proof. It cannot, however, afford to dispense with understanding. Religion lives from understanding, from the conscious commitment to ideas which illuminate experience and are morally fruitful. The entire point of this work is to suggest a new pattern of understanding at a time and in a climate where the consideration uppermost in everyone's mind is: What do you *mean* when you speak about such notions as God, sin, atonement in a secularized world? The new spirit of candor which has made its appearance on the contemporary religious scene is a salutary expression of dissatisfaction with the mere repetition of ancient formulas, both liturgical and theological, which have no point of contact with the experience of the modern world. The following chapters, therefore, represent an attempt to reinterpret some ancient formulas in terms of experience with the hope that they will seem less strange and that even those who cannot accept either the formulas or their reinterpretation will, nevertheless, be led to some understanding of what they mean for those who do accept them.

I

The Classical Meaning of
"Faith Seeking Understanding"

The ancient encounter of Christianity with classical culture, especially with the Greek philosophical traditions, has had a powerful influence on the shape of Christian faith and the destiny of the church in the world. Two significant factors stand out; one will be used as a focus for the ensuing discussion. In the first place, when the Fathers of the early church availed themselves of the language, the concepts and principles of the philosophical traditions for the elucidation of the Christian content, they clearly involved themselves in an ambiguous enterprise. For, while there can be no question that their approach bestowed a logical rigor and systematic clarity on the developing Christian theology, it is also true that they ran the risk of transforming biblical insight into something other than itself. And, although I do not agree with those who exaggerate this risk in order to dismiss philosophy as irrelevant, I do not underestimate the problem. There is no doubt, for example, that the emphasis on static perfection in Greek thought and the identification of God with such perfection sets up a tension with the Christian conception of a living God who does not stand aloof from man and the world but is present in the world. And yet despite the danger of distortion, no theologian ever has, or ever could, express Christian faith in a set of ideas wholly of biblical origin and entirely free of content derived from not only philosophy but other forms of secular thought as well.

The second consequence of the encounter with ancient philosophy is found in the conviction that Christianity is an intelligible faith, and that while we ever "see through a glass darkly, and not face to face," we can nevertheless probe the depths of Christian concepts and experiences in the quest for understanding. Faith, to be sure, precedes, but faith is not sheer belief in we know not what. In this regard Christianity was not a "mystery religion." On the contrary, the ancient theologians were concerned to express faith in a public and intelligible form, confident that the truth about God can be apprehended through similitudes based on the finite things of creation. Thus, from the beginning, the Christian content was *not* conceived as a wholly foreign body of thought, wholly discontinuous with human thought and experience and therefore opaque to understanding. There were, of course, differences of opinion among theologians as to what understanding the faith was to mean, as to how far understanding could go, and especially as to the precise contribution understanding was to make. But the fact remains that there existed a firm belief in the intelligibility of faith and in its power to show itself forth in the form of truth. It seems to me most unfortunate that so many theologians at present have abandoned this belief in intelligibility, preferring instead to accept modern skepticism according to which there is no truth in any sphere but that of the natural sciences; all else is opinion expressed through the language of some "style of life."

As a prelude to the development in the next chapter of a new approach to the ancient venture of understanding, let us analyze both the conception and the practice that lay behind the formula, *Faith Seeking Understanding,* which was itself rooted in the doctrine of *credo ut intelligam* ("I believe in order that I may understand"). Two theologians employed this formula to a greater extent and with more success than any others—Augustine of Hippo and Anselm of Canterbury. In approaching their explication of this formula, it is absolutely essential to keep in mind a clearly demonstrable historical fact having to do with the distinction between faith and reason in the so-called High Middle Ages. That fact is this: the point of development reached by theology at the time of Albert the Great and Thomas Aquinas required that a precise delineation be made between the spheres of reason and of faith. The particular reasons for this demand need not concern us. The disjunction of the two forms was effected, and their respective nonoverlapping tasks defined. This later development, however, must not be read back into the thought of either Augustine or Anselm, for as an examination of the relevant texts will show,[1] neither made a knife-edge distinction between faith and reason, thus locating them in noncommunicating compartments; both kept the two forms in suspension within the concept of Christian wisdom *(sapientia)*. Some writers, largely those who find the solution of Aquinas congenial, have found fault with Augustine and Anselm for the ambiguity in their positions that makes possible contradictory interpretations. And it is true that both thinkers can be interpreted as fideists or as rationalists, depending on how we construe the function of reason vis-à-vis the nonbeliever. [2]

Moreover, the position of both earlier thinkers enjoys an advantage over later theologies which presupposed the separation between reason and faith even if their position suffers from the ambiguity previously noted. When reason and faith are held in suspension and tension, reason is kept in creative relation to faith and is not sealed off or confined to the sphere of the "natural" standing over against the "supernatural" domain of faith. Once

1. For a clear and cogent examination of this point see M. J. Charlesworth, *St. Anselm's Proslogion* (Oxford, 1965), pp. 22–40. Charlesworth shows that (1) Anselm and Augustine are close to each other in their views of the relation between faith and reason, although neither thinker is without ambiguity on the topic; (2) neither thinker regarded it as essential to draw a clear and unambiguous distinction between faith and reason; (3) we misunderstand both thinkers if we read them against the background of later medieval thought when the spheres of faith and reason were sharply delineated.

2. The dual interpretation is more clear in the case of Anselm than Augustine because of some strong statements by the former in the *Cur deus homo?* concerning the power of reason to show the necessity of the Incarnation even for those who do not share certain Christian assumptions. There it is clear that Anselm did not confine the exercise of reason to its role *within* faith where it is to make explicit what is already grasped by faith. See M. J. Charlesworth, *St. Anselm's Proslogion*, pp. 30ff. On the other hand, Anselm also wanted to maintain the *credo ut intelligam* doctrine. Augustine never made as large a claim for reason's competence outside faith as Anselm did, but even he did not confine the office of reason solely within faith. See F. Copleston, *History of Philosophy*, II (Westminster, Md., 1946), p. 48 for a fine statement about the faith/reason ambiguity in Augustine.

the distinction was allowed to harden into a separation, the dynamic relation between faith and reason was lost. The two could no longer interpenetrate as they did in Augustine's quest for understanding. Instead, we have a logical distinction of spheres: to faith is awarded the mysteries of revealed theology beyond the competence of reason to discover or criticize, and to reason is awarded secular knowledge and the metaphysic of the natural intellect. The two spheres, though utterly distinct, are related through the principle that, having the same source in God (Truth), they cannot conflict with each other. But it is important to notice that the believing and questing self—the reflective and meditative self made central by the Augustinian tradition—in whose experience the interpenetration of faith and reason was contained has vanished. The dynamic interplay between faith and reason in the *temporal* experience of the individual was replaced by a distinction of spheres on an essentially *spatial* analogy. The dynamic element disappears. Faith is set above reason as its completion, and the two are related in tandem fashion; the sense that they interprenetrate in the experience and life of the believer is obscured.

The point just underlined is essential for understanding the *fides quaerens intellectum* formula as it was operative in the thought of its two greatest representatives. If both Augustine and Anselm left faith and reason in a somewhat ambiguous relation by comparison with the neatness of the Thomistic scheme, they nevertheless preserved the concreteness of individual experience as a living venture in which the man of faith is attempting through reason to discover the meaning of what he believes.

As is well known, the biblical foundation of the doctrine we are considering is found in the Septuagint version of Isaiah 7:9: "Unless you believe, you shall not understand."[3]Augustine's first proposition is that faith precedes understanding as walking by faith precedes sight. He says in his exposition of the Fourth

3. Augustine was aware of the other reading of this text, "unless you believe, you will not be established (abide)" and, in his characteristic generosity, he argued that each version brings us some truth. See *De doctr. Christ.* II.12, where he connects understanding with what abides and does not perish.

Gospel: "For we believe in order that we may know, we do not know in order that we may believe. . . ."[4] The faith here in question is to be understood in two senses. On the one hand, it means faith as *content* or the substance of the Christian understanding of God, man and the world which has been received in the form of sacred writings from the past. On the other hand, faith means also the *relation* of the individual to that content and to the God disclosed in it; at the outset he accepts it as true and is willing to trust it as a guide for his life. "When," says Augustine, "the mind has been imbued with the first elements of that faith which worketh by love (Galatians 5:6), it endeavors *by purity of life,* to attain unto sight. . . ."[5] Expressed here is that fundamental duality in the relational sense of faith which has played such a decisive role in the history of theology. Faith has its *cognitive* side expressed in the acceptance of the content as the truth. However, if that side is not to be reduced to "mere assent," there must be the *conative* side as well, the side that involves love and trust, the will to shape life in accordance with the content so that in the end "he who wills to do the Father's will, shall know" (John 7:17). The conative side brings in the essential factor of love, and the engagement of the person. The two sides are related as the beginning and end of a process; the cognitive side precedes, but at that stage, the person has no more than a logical or conceptual grasp of the content of faith; coming to know that content in a more vital sense (by "acquaintance") requires trust and participation in the form of life it entails.[6] Augustine was well aware of both sides of faith and he sought to keep them in balance.[7] That the thinkers of the later Middle Ages lost this balance is clear; they placed faith exclusively in the genus of the cognitive where it was forced to assume the status of a mean between opinion and

---

4. *Tractates on the Gospel of St. John* XL.9 in *Nicene and Post-Nicene Fathers,* Philip Schaff, ed. (New York, 1888), Vol. VII.

5. *Enchiridion* I.5 (italics added).

6. See *Tractates on the Gospel of St. John* XXXIX.6, where Augustine interprets John 7:17 in terms of the "believe in order that you may understand" formula.

7. See the essay "Faith and Reason" by R. E. Cushman in R. W. Battenhouse, ed., *A Companion to the Study of St. Augustine* (New York, 1955), pp. 287-314, and C. N. Cochrane, *Christianity and Classical Culture* (New York, 1944), ch. XI.

certain knowledge. It was, as we now understand so well, the momentous task of the Reformers to recover the conative side of faith in a return to personal experience and to put emphasis on the relation of the creature to God.

The question naturally arising at this point concerns the nature of understanding and its contribution to the religious relationship. Two pairs of distinctions are called for. To begin with, we must distinguish between understanding or intelligibility on the one hand, and proof or demonstration on the other. Second, we must take note of the difference between activity of reason *within* faith and that same activity as it appears *prior* to faith (see below pp. 9–16). These distinctions are relevant for both Augustine and Anselm but the two thinkers require separate treatment, for Anselm went considerably beyond his predecessor in the claims he made for reason operating beyond the ambit of faith. With regard to the first distinction, Augustine's conception of the quest for understanding clearly means a quest for intelligibility in which finite things and experiences ("things below") are seen as instrumental in leading the mind to grasp the transcendent truths ("things above")[8] Here it is not a question of a "natural theology" based on a demonstrative reason that has a wholly human foundation, since according to Augustine's doctrine of illumination—*in lumine tuo videbimus lumen*—all understanding is made possible through the illumination of the Uncreated Light. Instead, emphasis falls on the manner in which the finite or created things are capable of functioning as symbols and signs through which the divine can be understood. The only way in which we can hope to grasp the meaning of a content that transcends the horizon of man is by finding likenesses of it in knowledge of the world and human experience. It is characteristic of the illumination tradition stemming ultimately from Plato, that the mind be led to *see* the truth through similitudes and likenesses. This reflective and meditative approach, carried on by each individual for himself, stands in contrast to logical demonstration in which propositions are related to each other in accord-

8. See *De trin.* I.1.

ance with explicitly stated principles quite apart from reference to the experience of any individual person. There are, to be sure, passages in Augustine where we can find the now familiar demonstrative proofs for the existence of God, and to that extent we cannot deny that reason in the form of logical constraint or proof is present in his thought. If, however, we consider a work like *De trinitate,* which is in fact Augustine's most sustained exhibition of faith seeking understanding, we find not that reason makes available to us a logical proof of the existence of a trinitarian God, but that instead there is a reflective enterprise of understanding in which the several trinities of the human soul are seen as intelligible likenesses of the triune God. We do not start with these likenesses and deduce the Trinity; on the contrary, we start with the doctrine of the Trinity and attempt, through a reflective analysis of our experience of ourselves, to understand or show the intelligibility of what it means to speak of God as a trinity or community of persons. The result of such an analysis is not the discovery of the content of faith, but the discovery that that content is intelligible because it can be understood through similitudes found in the things of experience.

Still confining attention to the function of reason within the ambit of faith, we may go on to ask what contribution understanding makes, for if we are to believe in order to understand, the understanding, in whatever measure it is attained, must represent some sort of advance beyond our original position. It seems quite idle to suppose that faith with understanding is exactly the same thing as faith devoid of understanding.[9] There are, in fact, for Augustine two contributions made by understanding. First, it serves as a spur to seeking after God, and, second, it confirms the believer in his faith. In *De trinitate,* Augustine says:

---

9. I shall suggest below that there can be no absolute distinction between "mere" or "bare" faith and faith with understanding, because the initial grasping in faith of any content whatever requires that the process of understanding shall already have begun. In the end we have a distinction not between bare faith and faith with understanding, but between initial faith and that minimal understanding which keeps the content from being mere words or, worse, gibberish, and understanding as an explicit task or quest.

"And, yet again, understanding still seeks him whom it finds; for 'God looked down upon the sons of men,' as it is sung in the holy Psalm, 'to see if there were any that would understand, and seek after God.' And man, therefore, ought for this purpose to have understanding, that he may seek after God."[10] The point is important because it underlines both the dynamic and the experiential character of the process of understanding. The search for insight is not correctly described as a journey which leads away from the object of faith into some barren land of speculation, or as a vain and abstruse translation into speculative concepts of a reality previously apprehended as a living power. On the contrary, in Augustine's view, man is able to seek after what he already in some sense knows; the opening paragraphs of the *Confessions* make the point very well. "For it would seem clear," he writes, "that no one can call upon Thee without knowing Thee, for if he did he might invoke another than Thee, knowing Thee not."[11] Understanding, far from being a distraction from the search for God, appears as a constant incentive and a necessary guide to that search, a guide which alone can guard against the confusion of God with the creatures.

Understanding, moreover, confirms the believer in his faith by the discovery that it has its own intelligibility. God is truth and his nature is made manifest in and through the creation. Augustine frequently referred in this regard to Romans 1:20: "The invisible things of God, from the creation of the world are made visible by the works he has made." The movement of the mind toward understanding is a penetration into the depths of things divine; that movement saves the believer from acquiescing in a faith which is no more than acceptance of an unmediated and opaque authority. Faith, once again, precedes, but as understanding develops there arises a more intimate and personal apprehension through our own experience of the truth of faith.

10. *De trin.* XV.ii.2.
11. *The Confessions of St. Augustine*, F. J. Sheed, trans. (New York, 1943), I.i; cf. V.iii.

At every step progress is dependent on the illumination of the Uncreated Light.

Having sketched the fundamental form of reason operating *within* faith in the quest for understanding, some attention must be paid to Augustine's view of reason's operation beyond the borders of faith. In the first instance, it is clear that for Augustine the existence of reason[12] in man is what distinguishes him from other creatures. The philosophical analysis of the nature of time in the *Confessions* as well as the account of bodies, their properties and relations, and the theory of mathematics as intelligible truth all testify to what Augustine understood as the operation of reason apart from faith in any essentially religious sense. There are at least two places in his writings where Augustine goes beyond the view presented above and reaches the point of reversing the crucial antecedence of faith. In *De ordine*, an early work to be sure, he says: "In point of time, authority [i.e., faith] is first; but in the order of reality, reason is prior."[13] And it is clear from the context that he refers to progress in the quest for the understanding of faith which stems from rational analysis and reflection. Again in Epistle 120 he says: "So, therefore, if it is rational that faith precedes reason in the case of certain great matters that cannot be grasped, there cannot be the least doubt that reason which persuades us of this precept—that faith precedes reason—itself precedes faith."[14] In short, if man were not a rational being to begin with he could not grasp either the meaning of *credo ut intelligam* and *fides quaerens intellectum*, or see the superiority of these principles over other alternatives. And Augustine, as is evident in *De utilitate credendi*, argued the case against those who rejected his own formula that one must believe in order to under-

---

12. Here reason must not be understood in too narrow a sense; it means the ability to use language, to form concepts, to remember and indeed to perform all "intentional" acts—anticipation, hope, etc.

13. *De ord.* II.9.26. *Tempore auctoritas, re autem ratio prior est.*

14. I am indebted to Charlesworth, op. cit., p. 27, for this passage; the reader should consult also the passage translated from Sermon 126 in note 2 on the same page.

stand. The contemporary lesson to be derived from Augustine is that however far we may go in the direction of establishing utter discontinuity between the content of faith and human reason, we still must appeal to man's intelligence to grasp and appropriate that point itself. The entire discussion of the relation between faith and understanding or reason presupposes that reason is operative in the acceptance of any conclusion to which we may come.

It should be clear that Augustine's view of faith, reason and understanding is complex at the least, and on the edge of inconsistency, at the most. It is, however, clear that he founded his theological enterprise on the *credo ut intelligam* principle and that he consistently refused to accept the converse of that relationship; understanding is not necessary for believing in the first instance, but faith is necessary for understanding. There are no passages in Augustine's writings where he proposes to substitute understanding for faith at the outset. Understanding is the *fruit* of faith, and where reason precedes either in the sense that man's capacity for thought and the use of language is presupposed in the initial act of believing, or in the sense that reason is to "persuade" us in the acceptance of the *credo ut intelligam* formula itself, faith is still not replaced as a starting point. In the end, Augustine's quest moves from faith to the understanding and the intelligibility of faith as the things of God become clearer through knowledge of man and his experience. "Therefore lift up your mind," he writes, "use your eyes like a man, look at heaven and earth, look at the things that are made and look for the Maker; look at the things you see, and look for Him whom you do not see."[15]

In considering Anselm's views of faith, reason and understand-

15. Sermon 126, Charlesworth, op. cit., p. 27, note 2. Cf. the following from *De civ. dei* XI.ii: "For God speaks with a man not by means of some audible creature dinning in his ears, so that atmospheric vibrations connect Him that makes with him that hears the sound, nor even by means of a spiritual being with the semblance of a body, such as we see in dreams or similar states. . . . Not by these, then, does God speak, but by the truth itself, if anyone is prepared to hear with the mind rather than with the body." *Nicene and Post-Nicene Fathers*, Philip Schaff, ed. (Buffalo, 1887), Vol. II.

ing, two facts stand out. In the first place he accepts and extends Augustine's program of "faith seeking understanding," as is evident from his own account of the original titles he proposed for the works known to us as the *Monologium* and the *Proslogium.* In the preface to the latter work he writes: "I have given to each its title, the first being called *An Example of Meditation on the Meaning of Faith,* and the sequel *Faith in Quest of Understanding"*[16] (*Fides quaerens intellectum*). Second, Anselm goes beyond the horizon set by Augustine with respect to the power of reason in demonstrating the *necessity* of truths initially delivered by faith. A balance in favor of rationalism begins to become evident, especially in *Cur deus homo?,* where it appears that the Incarnation is not only intelligible, but that it can even be seen to be a necessary truth.

The *Proslogium* begins with the call to reflection and contemplation which serves as the distinguishing mark of the Augustinian tradition in theology. "Enter into the inner chamber of your soul, shut out everything save God and what can be of help in your quest for Him and having locked the door seek Him out" [Matthew 6:6].[17] Here we see again the choice of man as the one created being upon whom the mark of the Creator is most evident and whose being therefore can be used as a sign and symbol of the God whom we do not see.[18] The reflective introduction to the famous argument for God's existence that is to come must be taken seriously because it sets the context within which reason operates. Anselm, in retiring into himself, is led to reflect on man's being made in the divine image and he, like Augustine, links this acknowledgment with memory and strives to recover the divine presence through understanding and love. The image is, however, effaced through man's own doing and must be renewed before understanding is possible. By appealing to passages in a multitude of psalms, Anselm shows that this renewal coincides with the doctrine of illumination; the created light of

16. Charlesworth, op. cit. p. 105.
17. Ibid., p. 11.
18. Bonaventura, the last great Augustinian of the medieval period, expressed this point in his distinction between an *image* and a *trace.* All created beings bear traces of God, but only man exhibits the image.

man can understand God only in the Light which is Uncreated. At this point in the reflective inner dialogue Anselm reiterates the well-known principle based on Isaiah 7:9: "For I do not seek to understand so that I may believe; but I believe so that I may understand."[19] From this vantage point he launches the ontological proof for God. With the proof itself and its logic, we are not basically concerned; for our purpose the chief question is: What is understanding, and what contribution does it make? Understanding for Anselm means primarily conceptual apprehension, embracing the nature of the object in question and its existence or place in being. Thus he approaches his inquiry by calling attention to both points. "Grant me," he says, "that I may understand as much as you see fit, that you exist as we believe you to exist, and that you are what we believe you to be."[20] Understanding, then, includes an apprehension of both existence ("that") and essence ("what"), a consideration which is, as we know, of the utmost importance to the ontological proof. Further insight into the nature of understanding is gained from Anselm's distinction between two senses in which something can be thought. In the first sense something is thought when the word signifying it is thought; in the second sense something is thought "when the very object which the thing is, is understood." Philosophically speaking, Anselm's position represents that of ancient realism according to which understanding penetrates through and beyond language to a grasp of the object itself. Understanding, therefore, does not set its object at a distance or transform it into something "merely theoretical," but instead brings the self which understands into more intimate relation to what is understood.

It seems clear that insofar as reason is operating within the ambit of a faith that is received, it has the task of seeking an understanding that confirms the believer in his faith. For Anselm, the one who meditates on the content of faith and seeks to understand what it means actually enjoys the discovery of faith's intelligibility. I want to stress what I take to be the element of personal

19. Charlesworth, op. cit., p. 115.
20. Ibid., p. 117.

experience here involved. That element is sometimes overlooked because of an overemphasis on the universality implied in rational understanding. The fact is that the believer with understanding is able to answer for his faith; if he has cast it in rational form, such as Anselm did when he interpreted God through the formula "that than which a greater cannot be thought," then he is able to say to the skeptic or the nonbeliever what it is that he means and wherein consists the intelligibility of what he means. The believer, moreover, is able to say that *through his own experience of understanding,* carried out in a meditative way *which each must do for himself,* [21] he is delivered from dependence on mere authority. His believing is not based merely on the authority of an institution, of another human being, or even of the Bible itself. He has reached a point where he experiences the intelligibility of faith *for himself.* This intelligibility, nevertheless, does *not* replace faith as the primary stance of the believer, and it is quite artificial to suggest that if one were in possession of such understanding at the outset, it might then have taken the place of faith. For the belief is that the understanding in question is possible only on condition of the formula *"nisi crederis, non intelligas."* [22]

21. Anselm thought of both the *Monologium* and the *Proslogium* as the result of "silent reasoning within himself," and he even says that neither work "deserves to be called a book"; cf. Plato's *Phaedr.* 274C-277A.

22. On the other hand, it will not do to take Anselm's enterprise of faith seeking understanding, as Karl Barth would do, in a purely fideistic sense. (Karl Barth, *Fides quaerens intellectum, Anselms Beweis der Existenz Gottes,* [München, 1931]; Eng. trans., *Anselm: Fides Quaerens Intellectum,* [Richmond, 1960], p. 57.) Quite apart from the more rationalistic position Anselm clearly displays in the arguments of *Cur deus homo?,* it is clear that he regards the argument of the *Proslogium* as having logical transitions in it which are meant to be compelling for all who understand the meanings of the concepts involved and the logical structure of the argument. That the *Proslogium* is more than an explication—the drawing out or making conceptually clear in detail—of the meaning of one of the names of God, can readily be shown, both in the argument itself and in the way Anselm regards it in his disputation with Gaunilon. To begin with, Anselm means to assert, in both versions of the ontological proof, that there is a crucial logical consequence in the reasoning; that consequence is expressed in the proposition that it is not the case that anyone can claim both to use the term "God" intelligibly and to deny that the reality denoted by the term exists *in re.* And even if we speak of this logical consequence as the discovery by the one who reasons silently of the intelligibility of his faith rather than of its demonstration, the fact remains that the logical

The upshot of this discussion is that Anselm cannot legitimately be interpreted in a one-sided way. That he wanted to uphold the priority of faith over understanding in the tradition of Augustine is clear. On the other hand, it is equally evident that in the *Proslogium* and *Cur deus homo?* there is explicit argument intended to be rationally compelling, and in the case of the latter work especially, there is the additional claim that the argument holds even for those who do not accept Christian assumptions. Therefore, quite apart from theological commitments and on the grounds of historical evidence, Anselm cannot be seen exclusively as either a fideist or a rationalist. Both strains are to be found in his writings and if the balance is to be tipped in favor of either side it is difficult to see how one could support the purely fideist side as Barth wants to do. The interesting fact is that later interpreters regarded Anselm as an innovator precisely because of his appeal to reason and his tendency to underplay dependence on "authorities."

The second fact previously mentioned about Anselm's conception of the office of reason vis-à-vis faith, brings into view the other side of his thought, the side that expresses his rationalism and at the same time lays foundation for the position of Aquinas

consequence is present and is asserted by Anselm. We may even say that the "discovery" of intelligibility for the faith content in this case is the discovery that when one thinks (or analyzes) that content in a conceptual way it is seen to entail the consequence that the assertion of the nonexistence of God is self-contradictory.

Even if one were to argue that the context of Anselm's argument is that of "faith seeking understanding," and hence that the concept of God involved is derived from historical tradition, the projected logic of the argument cannot be ignored. For what Anselm finds in his attempt to "understand" the nature of God is that his nonexistence is not a real possibility. Anselm was, after all, as he expressly says, searching for "one single argument that for its proof required no other save itself, and that by itself would suffice to prove that God really exists." (*Proslogion*, Preface, Charlesworth, op. cit., p. 103.) Moreover, as Charlesworth has pointed out, Gaunilon, who was closer to the argumentative context than any modern interpreter, clearly assumes that the proof is put forward as a *rationally compelling argument* to be examined in its own terms. Anselm, in turn, responds to Gaunilon's objections by attacking them and defending his original argument. There is no indication on Anselm's part either that Gaunilon has misunderstood the intent of his argument or that he, Anselm, disagrees with Gaunilon's assumption that it is to be taken as a rational argument.

in which the Augustinian living tension between reason and faith was disolved by the clear delineation of the two spheres, and the assigning of exclusive roles for each. The extreme tension in Anselm's position is nowhere more fully evident than in the preface to *Cur deus homo?* As has been pointed out repeatedly, Anselm held fast to the *credo ut intelligam* doctrine, and he even affirms it in the opening chapter of Book I.[23] A new note, however, is struck by him when he speaks about replying to the objections of "infidels" who regard Christian faith as absurd and contrary to reason in such a way that "leaving Christ out of view (as if nothing had ever been known of him)" it would still be possible to prove by absolute reasons that no man could be saved without Christ. Here we have an unambiguous claim in behalf of reason's role *outside* the ambit of faith. And as if this claim itself were not strong enough, Anselm goes on to say that if nothing were known of Christ it would still be possible through reason and the citations of fact to show that the true end of man can be reached only by God becoming man. Claims of this sort exhibit Anselm's extreme rationalism and advance an office for reason that goes beyond that of explicating or understanding the content of Christian faith as something given.[24] The appeal to the hypothetical proposition "If nothing had been known of Christ" sets in motion that line of thought which ultimately led to the separation between reason and faith and the consequent discussions about how much of the Christian content reason might have been able to discover had it been allowed to work under its own aegis in some nonhistorical vacuum. I want to return to this point later on in connection with a proposal for a new way of interpreting the "faith seeking understanding" formula. For the present, I shall underline two impor-

23. Speaking of those who urged him to offer a rational proof of incarnation, Anselm says, "This they ask, not for the sake of attaining to faith by means of reason, but, that they may be gladdened by understanding and meditating on those things which they believe." *Cur deus homo?* in *St. Anselm, Basic Writings*, S.W. Deane, trans. (La Salle Ill., 1962), p. 178.

24. From a historical point of view, the larger claim which Anselm advances and which seems to take him beyond Augustine's meditative quest to the point of proof and explicit demonstration can be understood when we consider the increasing influence on him of Boethius and the logical tradition.

tant considerations that are focused by Anselm's endeavor. In the first place, in opening up the distinction between believers and nonbelievers, Anselm had to distinguish two corresponding functions for reason, one of which is appropriate for the believer and one for the nonbeliever. In the case of believers, reason furnishes an understanding which constitutes a *confirmation* of faith without being a substitute for it, while in the case of non-believers, reason furnishes a ground of *conviction* not itself based on initial faith. In the case of the believer, the pattern is believing in order to understand, whereas in the case of the nonbeliever the pattern is understanding in order to believe. At this point the Augustinian tension and the interpenetration of faith and reason in the living experience of the person is on the verge of dissolution.

Instead of a believer who, as a living person in the world, is always to some extent a nonbeliever seeking constantly to overcome his disbelief through the confirmation of understanding, and a nonbeliever who is potentially a believer if he can hear the Christian content and appropriate it, we have instead two distinct classes of individuals. The believer is *all* believer, and the nonbeliever is *all* nonbeliever, and the tension between faith and doubt which should be a component in the experience of all men and which is, in fact, the driving force of all living faith and thought, is superseded. As the gap between the two classes widens, and we see it at its widest on the current scene, the believer appears as one who is too easily shielded from his nonbelief by the fact that, despite his impetus to understand what he believes and thus confirm his faith, such a move is ultimately not necessary since he can always retreat to the circle of faith. The nonbeliever, on the other hand, is left without a sufficient challenge by Christian faith because he is led to see it not as a truth which has a claim on his understanding, but only as a doctrine to be accepted on faith in the sense of authority.

The human situation is distorted when a tension which belongs essentially to the structure of existence is resolved by distributing the elements in tension over two distinct classes of individuals. The tension between religious insight and the disclosures of science, for example, might be "resolved" by constructing two distinct and nonoverlapping classes of persons—men of faith and men of science, the former would be unconcerned with the challenges of faith stemming from scientific knowledge, while the latter would have no concern for the limitations of science to which the existence of religious faith points. The obvious difficulty with such resolutions is that there is no man whose entire business is faith and whose life is unaffected by scientific knowledge of the world, and there is no man whose sole business is science and who therefore has no concern for his own being and his ultimate destiny. The truth is that there is only one man, one existence, one experience embracing many dimensions and it falls to each individual to participate in these dimensions and relate them to each other in his own life.

To return directly to Anselm, the second consideration focused by what we have called his rationalistic side concerns the indispensable role that human reason has to play in the reception, the interpretation and the appraisal of the historic content of faith. As Augustine saw, there must be a role for reason in addition to its function of reaching understanding within the sphere of faith, since we have to be able to grasp and interpret the *credo ut intelligam* formula itself as over against alternative ways of relating faith and reason. Nor will it be illuminating to suggest that reason is relieved of its role since the formula is found in the Bible, because the latter is not self-interpreting and every attempt to interpret depends not only on the knowledge we bring with us, but also on our use of language and our knowledge of both its grammar and its logic. And since there is no more a Christian logic than there is a Christian physics, we are thrown back again on our human rational resources, limited and imperfect as they are. Anselm saw that in fact the enterprise of faith seeking understanding takes us beyond the making explicit of what is already given. Understanding brings into play a range of knowledge and experience that can come only from an acquaintance and interaction with the world not to be uniquely derived from any deposit of faith. When Jesus tells us that the man who tries to save his life through an ever-increasing material security

will lose it in comparison with the one who finds his life or
realizes himself in love and devotion, we think at once not only
of his life but of our own experience and the experience of others
in order to find what I shall call *analogues* of that truth in the
world. Or when Paul tells us that "the good I would, I do not ... "
we do more than read words in a text; in the very act of apprehending his meaning we are forced to think of our own experience for the purpose of finding a counterpart[25] to his experience in own encounter with the world. The point in both cases
is the same; upon hearing a proposed truth we compare the
experience to which it refers with our own experience in order
to see whether we can say that our experience is the same. We
do not merely read and accept a form of words purporting to
express some truth about the world and ourselves without con-
sulting the testimony of our pervasive experience. On the contrary, in every act of comprehension we are led inevitably to
consult that experience in order to understand what the truth
claim means and whether it is verified by what has happened in
our own case.

Now, one may object, is this not setting up our own experience
as a final criterion, a touchstone for judging the religious content? My answer is dialectical, that is, both Yes and No and this
sort of answer is legitimate if we can say in exactly what sense it
is both. The answer is Yes, insofar as we cannot do otherwise.
That is to say, insofar as our commitment to faith is to be more
than acceptance of the authority of a book or an institution, we
shall have to understand as far as possible *what* it is we are
committed to, and this we cannot do without recourse to our own
experience. Moreover, if our commitment is to be more substantial than it would be if we merely said, "I accept this truth because
it appears in the Bible, or because a divinely instituted church
certifies it," we shall have to realize its meaning and find some
ground for its validity in our own experience. For it is one thing

25. Where the matter concerns the activity of God or transcendence we shall
speak of *analogues* in our experience in order not to confuse our experience with
its transcendent meaning; where the matter concerns the activity or experience
of man, vis-à-vis other men, we shall speak of *counterparts.*

to know that Paul has *said,* "The good I would . . ." and another for me to say the same words based now upon a recognition that they correctly express my situation. In the second case I am claiming something about present existence and not only that a man who lived in the past has made a certain pronouncement. On the other hand, and it is here that Anselm went too far, the answer to our question is No; to seek for an analogue or a counterpart in experience for some part of the religious content is not the same as supposing that, *if we had never received that content,* we might nevertheless, on the basis of reason and experience alone, have produced, deduced or anticipated it in the first place. In that case we would be setting up our own experience as a final criterion.

The distinction is crucial and it takes us back to my reference to Anselm's proposal that reason operate in a nonhistorical vacuum by asking what we could or could not show to be necessary with regard to the Christian content if we began by supposing that we had never heard of it. It is one thing to consider the *source* of a doctrine, an idea, an experience, and quite another to seek for its interpretation and its relation to pervasive experience. A clear parallel with the situation in empirical science is instructive. In order for a hypothesis to be tested or subjected to critical scrutiny, it must first be proposed. And those acquainted with the logical structure of the scientific enterprise know that the canons and procedures required for testing a hypothesis do not provide us with the necessary means of proposing it in the first place. An active, creative and synthetic imagination is required for that. Only after a proposal has been formulated can it be interpreted and considered critically in relation to actual experience.

In the religious situation it is not different. There is a deposit of faith, a content and tradition of revelation that stands as a historic fact and defines the religious community. The problem is to interpret it, understand it and relate it to pervasive experience; no one of these operations has to do with answering the question: Could we have discovered this content if we had searched for it by pure reason and apart from historical experience? The older contrast between a wholly natural order over which reason is sovereign, and a supernatural order known or apprehended through a form of revelation entirely discontinuous with both man and nature, must give way to a more empirical, historical understanding of the relationship between the world of the finite and God. The proper distinction to be drawn is between the revelatory significance attached by a historical community to certain crucial historical persons and events, on the one hand, and pervasive or repeatable experience that may be realized at any time or place because it does not form the exclusive substance of any one community's historical life. If the theological doctrines of creation and incarnation are taken seriously, intelligible relations must hold between finite reality and the transcendent reality at every point. For both doctrines involve the communication between God and the world, and no reality can be immanent in another if there is no point of identity between them. Two entirely heterogeneous realities can be related only externally in conjunctive form and signified by the term "and," but such a relationship is quite different from the immanent togetherness when one reality is "with" another. Conjunctions are notoriously promiscuous; the connective "and" is without restriction ("numbers *and* angels *and* nations," etc.) and even existential conjunctions, as bare conjunctions, may connect almost anything under the sun. For two realities, however, to be more intimately related than conjunction allows, for them to be *with* each other as body is with mind, meaning is with language, husband is with wife, the two cannot be "wholly other." In short, the revelatory sphere of special history cannot be wholly discontinuous either with the nature of the finite being who is to receive it or with the finite experience and language through which he must express and interpret it. The ultimate source of the Christian content, its revelatory matrix, is already *with* man's reason, his experience and his language in the sense that without these necessary conditions in finite existence, the record of the revelatory situation and the interpretation already present in its reception would not have been possible.

What may be overlooked at this point, however, is the *historical* character which human reason must assume. Not only must human reason manifest itself in a historical situation and context, but—and this is what Anselm overlooked—the content of faith is misconceived if it is regarded as a set of truths with no essential relation to the historical medium and the peculiar constellation of historical persons and events through which the biblical communities first apprehended them. The historical nature of the disclosure of God at the base of Christian faith is not mere appearance or external trapping. The historical medium itself is internally related to the religious content which it bears. One might think of a comprehensive scientific law—for example, one of the ideal-gas laws—or a fundamental theory such as universal gravitation as in principle[26] discoverable at any time assuming that the basic structure of the universe does not change from one cosmic epoch to another, but it is difficult to see what could be meant even by the supposition that the persons, the events and the experiences—Moses, Jesus, Paul—involved in revelation could have been discovered, or could now be discovered, by a reason operating in a vacuum. The fine-structure constant can be deduced, but not the historical continuum and its revelatory message. That message, like a scientific hypothesis, *once it is delivered or proposed,* can be analyzed, interpreted and subjected to critical scrutiny, but unless we suppose that the content of faith is a body of ideas totally independent of historical experience, it makes no sense to ask whether, if we were to treat that experience as either unknown or nonexistent, we might have discovered its truth by an appeal to reason and experience taken absolutely.

As a prelude to a new interpretation of the enterprise of "faith seeking understanding," it will be helpful to sum up the lessons to be learned from the classical conception we have reviewed. First, Augustine and Anselm were essentially correct in their insight that, while faith precedes reason, a living faith aware of itself in the world cannot remain dogmatic but must seek under-

26. It is obvious that the assumption behind "in principle" here coincides with the proposition that the historical situation, the state of science and scientists at a given time, etc., can safely be neglected or regarded as vacuous vis-à-vis a domain of timeless truth.

standing. If we look more closely at the situation we can see that "sheer" faith is a limiting concept; it is not possible to accept, believe, commit oneself to formulas entirely opaque or devoid of meaning. One can say the words "I believe in God," for example, but without some minimal grasp of what they are supposed to mean, one cannot actually believe what one says. All faith as such is *incipient* understanding, and we must replace the older distinction between "bare" or "simple" faith and faith confirmed in understanding with the distinction between faith endowed with that minimal understanding needed for any of its items to be *more* than a form of words associated with a context of piety, and the quest for explicit understanding which is aware of both itself and its goal.

Second, Augustine and Anselm were correct in their view that understanding means the discovery of the intelligibility of faith through similitudes, analogues and counterparts drawn from finite experience of the world and ourselves. The fruit of understanding, as both theologians realized, is confirmation in faith which is also the ground for a critical dialogue with other positions and points of view. On this account, understanding transcends the explication of the received content; it is more than a process of clarification. Involved as well is an appeal to finite experience and knowledge as a means of indicating how far faith coincides with pervasive experience. Moreover, the quest for understanding leads us to ask how a given doctrine is to be related to the rest of what we know about both nature and man derived from secular study. Anselm may have gone too far in his claim that, for example, the necessity of Incarnation could be shown on rational grounds alone, but he surely was not wrong in his bold attempt to show that the Christian content has its own logicality and is far indeed from being a body of arbitrary ideas that have no intelligible relation to the structure of existence.

The need, however, for a new approach to "faith seeking understanding," is pointed up by several inadequacies in the treatment of its two most eminent representatives. First, neither fully grasped the historical character of both faith and reason, the historical character of the revelatory content and the historical situation in which it was received. Consequently, their conception of reason was too narrow and not sufficiently responsive to change and development. Just as we no longer view the universe from the standpoint of a first-century cosmology, we no longer view reason as actualizing itself independently of historical circumstances in the recovery of timeless truths. Logic, moreover, has its own internal development and the canons of thought have changed numerous times in the period extending from the death of Augustine to our own century.[27] It is clear that modern logic with its mathematical bias and its loss of the philosophical relevance undoubtedly possessed by classical logic and even by the logic of Hegel is less available for theological and metaphysical thought than might be desired. We must take these changes seriously even if they appear to work against our enterprise; otherwise we fall into that irrelevance which characterizes a stagnant faith.

Second, while Augustine was remarkably sensitive to the nuances of man's experience and was, unlike Anselm, less inclined to play the role of the logician, both failed to take the full range of experience seriously. Of course, neither had the benefit of coming face to face with the appeal to experience which has dominated Western thought since the period of Enlightenment. Nor could either easily have understood the dialectic of experience that has passed from classical British empiricism through the criticism of Kant and Hegel to the reworking of what experience is and means at the hands of the pragmatists, the phenomenologists and the philosophers of existence. Both Augustine and Anselm placed too much emphasis on the individual meditating within the confines of his own mind: experience has a social as well as a personal dimension. Important as the contemplative stance may be, it does not exhaust our relation with reality. Experience means being in the world, it involves

27. It should not be thought that the point is merely academic or that developments in logic make no difference to theology. Protestants, especially, should not make this mistake in view, for example, of the crucial role played by the new nominalism in helping to formulate the importance and reality of the individual at the time of the Reformation.

interacting with the world and it embraces all that is ingredient in human community and history. Experience is more than contemplation and reflection; it is a many-sided interaction between man, the symbolic or language-using animal, and all that is to be encountered. The importance of experience in modern thought must be taken seriously because it furnishes us with a richer and more complex form of *understanding* than is possible on the basis of reflective reason alone. Experience does not exclude reason after the fashion of narrow and essentially nonempirical conceptions of experience; experience without interpretation is dumb. Experience transcends reason in concreteness and is therefore the matrix within which all understanding takes its rise. Religion, moreover, is at the center of experience and vice versa; it is impossible for them to be separated from each other. In the following chapter, I hope to show in the form of what I call the *analogia experientiae* how a new project of faith seeking understanding can be carried out which has experience at its center.

II

A New Approach to Understanding:
Analogia experientiae

The experience which forms the substance of every individual's life goes beyond what anyone can understand and consolidate within the confines of that experience itself. For this reason we are constantly working up hill, so to speak, seeking to understand and interpret what has already happened to us; and more often than not, the implications of present experience come to light only decades and even centuries later. In this sense the present is of vital importance for the past. I shall suggest in what follows that Protestantism, as represented by the experience of Luther or Calvin or Jonathan Edwards, had implicit within itself a fundamental insight which was not fully understood by any of these individuals in their own time.

Thus far our discussion of faith seeking understanding has focused on the contribution made by the Augustinian tradition and its representatives. The question now arises: How did the Reformers and their successors deal with the problem of relating understanding or reason to faith? Was there a characteristic continuation of the classical approach, did Protestantism attempt a fresh approach, or did it recast the problem entirely? To answer such questions fully would require an extended historical and theological account. There is, however, an important aspect of the subsequent development which needs to be accentuated on its own account and without reference to the theological controversy about the competence of human reason and the possibility of natural theology. That aspect is summed up in the proposition that the Reformers discovered the role of *experience* as the key to understanding in religion. Augustine was not unaware of the resources of experience for illuminating religious concepts and doctrines, but from his vantage point he could not grasp the significance of *individual* experience to the extent that became possible for the leaders of the Reformation coming on the scene, as they did, when the modern conception of the individual was in the making.

No one can understand and take seriously the decisive role played by the personal experience of a Luther or a Jonathan Edwards in apprehending the Christian message without also acknowledging the validity of this demand that there be intelligible relations between the concepts of theology and patterns of individual experience and behavior. The contrast between the theological past inherited by these men and their own encounter with conscience and the sense of separation from God is remarkable. Late medieval Aristotelianism in theology was marked by an analytical detachment and an emphasis on logical form which, despite the sanity of its rationality, nevertheless failed to do justice to the properly religious and experiential import of the Christian content. By comparison, the Reformers exhibited a dramatic change of context for understanding. Personal experience and religious concern were made central; the metaphysical and cosmological dimensions of theology were reduced in importance. There is a crucial truth in this experiential emphasis even if Protestantism's uneasiness about secular philosophy prevented it from providing such grounding for experience as would keep it from being set over against the physical world as something merely "subjective," human and evanescent. The apprehension and appropriation of the Christian content for the Reformers was not primarily a matter of citing authorities or summing up traditions, but rather, of self-examination and the analysis of experience in the light of theological ideas. In understanding the being of Christ, for example, in terms of the faith which justifies, Luther established an essential connection between the experience of the individual and the meaning of a basic theological doctrine. Similarly, Calvin, in his claim that the essence of the Lord's Supper is found in what the individual carries away with him "in the vessel of faith," was further paving the way for an experiential understanding of a central theological concept. The turn, moreover, taken by their thought in the direction of experience was itself indicated by their own experience. They did something more than propose a new logical alternative to previous ways for achieving understanding such as, for example, Aquinas had in mind when he dismissed the Augustinian illumination theory on the ground that all knowledge is sense-bound so that the first principles no longer point to the divine presence, but belong only to the created intellect. The Reformers entered their òwn experience as evidence of the failure of the previous institutional system of contrition and penance, and concluded that man's relation to God cannot be understood in these terms. It is one thing to argue on the basis of texts and authorities that a given interpretation of faith and justification is invalid because it distorts the biblical picture of Christ or fails to accord with the Pauline theology; it is quite another to discover for oneself that the objective system for appropriating what was called the merit of Christ developed by the medieval church leaves the human predicament unresolved.[1] Neither Luther nor Calvin could find within themselves an experience of divine acceptance through institutional absolution. Something else was required, something that could at once transcend the system of mediated grace and gain entrance to their own lives.

This, I take it, is what is both novel and essential in the appeal to experience that was to lead to the writing of a new chapter in the history of Christianity. Unfortunately, the new appeal was not consolidated as it should have been, partly because the proper concepts and principles were lacking for elaborating a theory, a metaphysic, of experience, and partly because classical Protestantism gave itself over so completely to a new rationalism of creeds. With the development of a new scholasticism, experience was set aside. But this later development should not obscure the role played by *experience* and *conscience* in determining the decisive

1. See Jonathan Edwards, *Religious Affections*, J. E. Smith, ed., Vol. 2, Yale ed., *Works of Jonathan Edwards* (New Haven, 1959), p. 452, for a remarkable statement about experience and what he called "experimental religion."

step taken by Luther and Calvin when they rejected previous interpretations. Two considerations are paramount: first, the appeal to experience meant a *trying out,* an actual attempt to live through[2] the cycle of contrition and penance, so that each could truthfully say, "the traditional way of understanding justification before God has been *tried* and found wanting." The important point is that, while all experience must remain subject to the interpreting word, it nevertheless exercises a *critical* function since the individual makes a discovery for himself. He does something more than consult a text or compare doctrinal statements; he experiences, in the sense of undergoing or suffering and living through, a series of personal events, and in the end he comes up against the failure of the confession and penance cycle. Of course, one may say that the interpretation of the experience was guided throughout by the biblical concept of justification by faith, and this is true, but it is also true that in the cases before us the discovery that one approach fails while the other succeeds is something more than the claim that the traditional penance doctrine is not biblical while the faith doctrine is. In short, justification by faith is mediated through experience in the sense that its meaning in human life has now made itself clear. We pass beyond knowing that a certain doctrine is supposed to mean this or that as expressed in accordance with texts and theological systems and reach an experience of exactly *what* it does mean. This is not to say that the interpreting word plays no role; it is to say that the experiential discovery of the meaning of a doctrine is not the same as reading about that doctrine in a book. A fact which, in turn, implies that both the Bible and its interpretation in tradition must be understood as mediating elements pointing to relations between God and man which still need to be realized in experience. Merely knowing that a doctrine has a certain conceptual content and merely holding correct doctrines are not enough; there remains the actual undergoing of the experience to which

2. Luther's experience is better known, of course, for Calvin was notoriously reticent, but, as John McNeill points out, it is impossible to read Calvin's *Reply to Cardinal Sadoleto* (1539) without becoming acutely aware of the personal experience that underlies the work.

the doctrine points. And yet the ironic note is that the various traditions of Protestantism, though thoroughly dependent on this experiential discovery and appeal of the Reformers, lost confidence in experience and failed to develop a theory of its nature and status that would serve to show its objectivity as a valid medium of understanding. Under the pressure of the problems posed by the phenomenon of "enthusiasm," and the polemical attack on Lutheranism, especially the charge that it was based on the merely "private" experience of one man, Protestantism often took refuge in new forms of the very rationalism against which its founders revolted. The result was a loss of the experiential medium in favor of the primacy of the creeds and of correct doctrine derived from a largely unimaginative exegesis of the Bible.

Despite the popular view of Protestantism as essentially evangelical, appealing to the heart and to the emotions, the fact is that the Reformed churches have been, on the whole, quite rationalistic in tone. They have combined a strict concern for correct doctrine with a not inconsiderable moralism which tends to exclude individual experience and runs the risk of losing intelligible relation to man's actual situation in the world as well. What is needed, and not only for the revitalization of Protestantism, but for the future life of Christianity, is a means of consolidating the appeal to experience which the Reformers discovered. For theirs was a new chapter in the long quest for an understanding of Christian faith. And their approach is not only well founded in the historical concreteness of the Judeo-Christian tradition, but it is admirably suited for application on the current scene and in the future that opens before us, since it is to man-in-the-world— the secular world—that the classical Christian message is to be spoken. That man is one whose consciousness has been shaped by a world of experience and it is only in and through *that* world that he can come to understand anything at all. Therefore, if the Christian conceptions are not to fall on deaf ears, or, worse still, remain uncommunicated because they are cast in a form which no one understands, we shall have to attempt to express their meaning in experiential terms. To this end I propose, first, to set

forth in general outline a fresh approach to faith seeking understanding through what I call the *analogia experientiae,* or experience as a language for theology, and second, to clarify the meaning of experience itself, its general shape and status in reality, in
order to correct the widespread impression that experience is
merely a tissue of subjectivity or a domain of privacy.

As we saw earlier in the discussion of the classical program of
"faith seeking understanding," Christian thinkers have long seen
the truth that the understanding of faith requires an interpreting
medium of some kind. Insofar as Christianity is not essentially
mysticism in which all mediating elements are transcended, a
medium of expression, a language, is required if we are to be able
to say what a given doctrine means. That is to say, when we speak
of God, in the nature of the case, we always must speak at the
same time of some *other* in and through which the nature of God
is supposed to be disclosed. The Augustinian theologians, following the principle that the created things provide us with signs,
symbols and analogues of the God who created them, were inclined to use the classical philosophical language of Being for this
mediating function. The Reformers, as we know, were critical of
this ontological approach and proposed instead to make the language of the Bible serve as the other, or mediating element.
However, as we know, that language itself, and the experience
expressed through it, must be interpreted; it is my proposal that
this interpreting be done through the finding of analogues in
human experience itself. This is the reason I speak of an *analogia
experientiae.* What is meant, however, is not some form of natural
theology in which we begin *de novo* with religious experience, so
called,[3] but rather, the use of experience as a means of understanding a faith content that is by no means derivative from such
experience. It is, for example, one thing to propose to derive a
theological concept such as that of atonement from experience,

3. In *Experience and God* I criticized the concept of religious experience because
I believe it is based too exclusively on the model of the classical conception of
experience as the passive reception of data as "given." I stressed instead what I
call the religious dimension of experience as that sphere of meaning in which we
are concerned with the ground and goal of our existence taken as a whole.

and quite another to attempt, given the concept itself, to find analogues within experience which would serve to provide understanding of what such an idea could mean to us in our actual existence. The latter enterprise is what I have in mind when I speak of the *analogia experientiae.* The use of such analogy, moreover, is inescapable, and for two basic reasons, one logical and the other religious.

The logical reason has already been considered; we need only repeat the point that to speak intelligibly of *theos* requires a *logos* and even if we say that the *logos* required is furnished by the figure of Christ and the biblical record, we shall still need a further *logos* by means of which to interpret both. The religious reason has to do with the dialectic between faith and doubt. Wherever there is living faith possessed by a person who lives in the world and is aware of its many dimensions, that faith is not shielded from doubt and uncertainty in advance but actually derives its life and dynamic force from a continual overcoming of doubt. When confronted with an item of faith, we want first to know what it means; and second, we want to know to what extent it is exhibited in and intelligibly related to our experience. To fail to ask these questions posed by the precariousness of our existence and the undeniable challenge to faith presented by the thought patterns of our secular world is to fall back on some form of authoritarianism. It is to suppose that the content of faith, which indeed we have only and always in earthen vessels, is to be preserved by bare repetition (i.e., by reciting a creed or citing biblical passages in response to questions) without criticism and without reinterpretation. The quest for analogues of faith is at the same time a quest initiated by living faith for the means of overcoming doubt by attaining a sense that our faith is grounded in the structure of what there is, and is therefore more than self-indulgence or wishful thinking. If, however, experience is to perform this function, we shall need a theory of its generic character and some assessment of its status in reality. For as long as it continues to be believed that experience is a merely subjective mental content, or that it is a purely human fabric entirely dependent on man, its essential role in religion—including the role which it played throughout biblical history and in the careers of the Reformers —will not be taken seriously.

All experience may be considered from two distinct but related standpoints; on the one hand, we have it or live through it in the form of its specific content; it is experience of this person, of that landscape, of that sense of alienation from God, of that peace which passes understanding. On the other hand, we can view experience generically as having a recurrent structure and as having a certain status in reality. In short, there are experiences and there is a theory of the nature and status of experience. In the end it is the specific experiences that are paramount and, as we shall see, must serve as the analogues for understanding what is meant by God. But the theory of experience must not be ignored, because, if experience reaches no further than the sphere of sensible objects, it is evident that there would be no point whatever in talking about the experience of, or the encounter with, God. Or again, if it were supposed that all experience is of what is wholly "immanent" or finite, the possibility of encountering a transcendent reality would be ruled out at the start, and if this is so we should be able to trace that consequence to its proper source in the theory of experience with which we set out. Therefore, though I do not argue that we cannot *have* experiences without also having before us a theory of experience, I would maintain, however, that such a theory is absolutely necessary—and is, in fact, always presupposed—for the critical interpretation and appraisal of any experiences had.

The appeal to experience and the systems of empirical philosophies have dominated Western thought since the eighteenth century. While, it is true, Aristotle spoke of the "empirical" physicians by which he meant those who were actually acquainted with a case of a particular ailment and who "knew how" to do something to effect a cure, it was for Locke and his successors to formulate the basic principles that define empiricism among Anglo-Saxon philosophers. Classical British empiricism, however, is not the only account that has been given of experience in modern thought—even if it has become the hallmark of what it means to make experience the basis of all thought. There is the theory developed by the American philosophers—Peirce, James and Dewey—influenced by some fundamental notions first set forth by Kant and Hegel. It is the latter position—what I call the reconstructed conception of experience—which I believe is most adequate for religious and theological purposes. On the other hand, this view was developed in conscious opposition to the position held by the classical empiricist philosophers and it is of the utmost importance to make explicit the crucial differences between the two positions. That such a distinction is no mere academic exercise can be seen from the fact that the British version of empiricism has been largely responsible for the view, especially prevalent among some recent Protestant theologians, that experience is insubstantial, unstable, evanescent and, in the end, a tissue of subjective interests and feelings. It is this largely derogatory and, as I hold, essentially erroneous, view of experience which has stood in the way of our being able to give to it its proper and indispensable role in religious insight.

There are three points of contrast between the conception of experience that derives largely from the British empiricists and still survives in much contemporary philosophy, and what I would regard as a more faithful account of the nature and status of the experience we actually have. First, there is the contrast between experience as the domain of sense—sense qualities and sensible things—and sharply distinguished from reason or thought, and experience understood as the funded and meaningful result of a multidimensional encounter between a concrete person and whatever there is to be encountered. Second, there is the contrast between experience as a body of data present to a theoretical observer who regards the *knowing* of those data as the primary concern, and experience in its variety embracing the moral, esthetic, scientific and religious dimensions which give point and purpose to the life of an individual person. Third, there is the contrast between experience seen as a private mental content which stands as a veil between ourselves and the so-called external world, and experience as an objective disclosure of what is there to be encountered, whatever it may prove to be. After considering these contrasts in some detail, we must go further and point out the status of experience in reality, seeing it as an emergent and irreducible medium that results from the interaction between what is and the symbol-using animal who can apprehend and interpret it. The capacity of experience to function as the language of theology and to be used as the *analogia experientiae* is ultimately dependent on its having the status of an objective disclosure of things.

According to the classical view, experience is coextensive with the domain of what can be sensed, and as a consequence the material of experience was analyzed into the qualities—colors, sounds, odors, tastes and tactile sensations—that correspond to man's sensory apparatus. Although it has been argued by some that this view does not entail a thorough-going atomism, it still cannot be denied that it exhibits a tendency in that direction. For the aim in view is the discovery of the precise and simple sensory data that underly all of our conceptions and beliefs. Experience so understood forms a contrast domain to rational thought and when it is made to serve as a touchstone for testing our complex beliefs, the result is that any reference in these beliefs to God, to the intentional center of a person, to freedom or to obligation must mean reference to what goes beyond experience. For having identified experience with the deliverances of the standard senses, the proponents of this view are forced to demand either that the sense data underlying the foregoing conceptions be produced, or to claim that they have no referents in experience at all.[4] Insofar as we cannot think of the concepts previously mentioned, and many others, as referring to objects analyzable into sensible data, we are left with the conclusion that what we mean to talk about when we use these concepts is entirely beyond experience. The upshot is that experience, so understood, becomes irrelevant to religion, and indeed to other regions of life involving forms of meaning not obviously reducible to references to the data of sense.

But, we may reasonably ask, What is the basic justification for

4. I have sought to develop this point at some length in *Religion and Empiricism* (Milwaukee, 1967).

analyzing the nature of experience in this way? All of our encounters with the world, other persons, and indeed our own selves, surely involve sensory content, but it does not follow from this fact that our encounters, what they are and what they mean, can be adequately construed merely by pointing to clear-cut sensible data. To take but one characteristic example: when two persons are engaged in conversation, each is attempting to grasp what the other is attempting to say and to this end each attends to the words and gestures of the other. The presupposition in every conversation is that these words and gestures are intelligible and can be interpreted because they are the expression of a center of intention or purposive unity which constitutes that person as one self. That unity, however, in the case of each self is not identical with any sensible datum had by either self. The words they hear, and the gestures they see; the unity of the self expressed through sound and sight is neither seen nor heard. On the classical view that unity, being beyond sense, is also beyond experience; I do not "experience" the other in his integrity as a person, I experience only the variety of his sensory activity. And yet, as I would insist, that sensory activity can be interpreted meaningfully only insofar as it is taken in the first place as the expression of the personal center. That center is ingredient in the sensory activity and if the latter is experienced, so is the former, even if we have to reject the identity of experience with sense experience in order to make the point.

Classical empiricism not only encounters difficulties in interpreting a complete unity like the person, but, in its emphasis on sense content, it fails to see that experience is not only its identifiable content, but has, as well, meaning dimensions within itself which express our purposes and aims in interpreting and evaluating it. The same content of experience can be taken, as William James put it, many times over. The tree standing on a gently sloping hillside will be considered by the lumberman as yielding so many board feet for the sawmill, whereas the poet may see it as a lonely sentinel standing guard over the meadow rolling beneath. The man of faith, experiencing the same tree, will see it as a creature and as a part of an order of creation brought forth by the God whom Moses encountered on the holy mountain. The sensory content remains invariant for all three persons and yet the meaning is very different for each. If, however, experience is no more than the sensory content they share, the different dimensions of meaning which are undeniably present for each individual must be banished from the world or confined entirely to the mind of the one who has the experience. On the latter alternative the world itself is deprived of the full depth of meaning which it reveals—moral, esthetic, religious—and it is supposed instead that man simply "adds" this meaning through his own mind and feeling to an otherwise "neutral" material. Another way of expressing this point is to say that a fully adequate expression of experience is impossible as long as we identify it with its sense content and set it off in contrast to thought and understanding. The two elements always interpenetrate in every experience; we encounter a situation shot through with sensory features, but we are not passive recipients who merely register or copy these features; we apprehend, grasp, understand and interpret in accordance with many meaning patterns. Were it otherwise, human experience would be no more than the results to be attained through mechanical apparatus, cameras, tape recorders and thermometers. To say that the sensory contents are "really there" while the meaning patterns are all supplied by the mind is to falsify experience as we have it. The content and the meaning are always together and while we can distinguish the two elements we cannot separate them without distortion.

With regard to the second contrast, the classical empiricists turned experience into knowledge for a theoretical observer who abstracts from the basic fact that he is a concrete person who stands in many relations to the world he seeks to know; knowing that world as an observer is only one of these relations. Not only is man as knower elevated on this view to a position of importance beyond all the other stances and purposes of life, but the world, including other selves, appears as nothing more than a body of phenomena to be explained in scientific terms. It is in this way that the world comes to be reduced to a collection of "objects" which we merely observe; these objects lose their interiority and value in themselves because their entire being consists in their being known by a knower who hopes to control their behavior by understanding how they "work." That we confront the world with many aims in view and that we do not always look upon it exclusively as material for theoretical knowing gradually comes to be forgotten. The theoretical bias becomes so firmly established that no other alternatives are envisaged; knowledge becomes coextensive with reality so that, by comparison, our other purposes in relation to the world and ourselves are made to seem secondary, insubstantial and thoroughly subjective.

The error here is a failure to understand that the one who experiences is a person who lives in his experience and whose experience constitutes his life. As persons we participate in or are engaged in the world; we see it as the scene of self-realization. Unlike Apollo, we cannot find our whole being in observing the world or in contemplating it from a safe distance. We do not live merely for the purpose of knowing the world, although there are those who imply that we do when they speak, usually extravagantly, about a life of science. Knowledge in the paradigm form of science is, to be sure, one of the preeminent forces in modern life, but as Dewey, who was a lifelong defender of scientific method, pointed out, the world as disclosed in theoretical knowledge represents but one of the modes in which experience manifests itself. Experience embraces many situations—moral, esthetic, economic, legal, religious, among them—in which our primary concern is not that of explaining the world theoretically; in these situations the one who experiences them has an active interest and involvement, a concern and a care, which manifest his own being as transcending his role as a knower. The experiences we undergo make up the meaningful content of our lives; in and through them we are realized. And while every item and aspect of what we experience can be made material for knowledge and science, it is by no means exhausted by that fact. Experience is meaningful life and only a mistaken view could lead us to regard experience as a sort of Midas touch turning all that we encounter, and all that we do, into material for theoretical explanation.

The modern philosophers of existence have understood the problem best. Hence they contrast detachment with passionate involvement. In Kierkegaard's example, a man may, as possessor of theoretical knowledge, repeat with a show of certainty, the ancient proposition "All men are mortal" without being acutely aware that it means, in part, "I, too, must die." And with this recognition we see not only our own involvement in experience, the question of our own goal and destiny, but we become aware as well of the present in which we exist and of the future stretching precariously before us. When experience is understood as no more than the observation of finished fact, it is reduced to the propositions of the past, to concern with what has been. But as living beings of care and involvement we are confronted by the present and oriented to the future. We seek constantly to know what our experience means to us and for us, and, more, we attempt to discover what is demanded of us in relation to ourselves, other selves and society. Viewing what we suffer and undergo as if we were merely passive spectators is precisely what may stand in the way of our grasp of its implications for ourselves as beings who are not finished, but who must still strive in a world of peril, of evil, of contingency overshadowed by the possibility of cosmic destruction.

In view, therefore, of the many dimensions of meaning ingredient in experience and the fact of its crucial importance for the individual whose experience it is, we must no longer think of experience solely as material for science and theoretical knowledge. Experience has as well a decisive significance for religion, for art, for morality, and indeed for all the essentially spiritual dimensions of human life.

This brings us to the third contrast, that between experience as an immediate mental content which somehow stands between ourselves and the external world, and experience as an objective means of disclosing the world about us. More damage has been done to the status of experience by the belief that it is essentially mental and present immediately to the individual than by any other empiricist doctrine. Without going into the many reasons involved, we can expose the main point, namely, that experience is supposed to be in some peculiar sense self-reflexive; it is supposed to be *experience of itself* and not of the realities that present themselves for encounter. This belief and this belief alone has led so many to regard experience as "subjective," a tissue of private, mental appearances that are not identical with the so-called external reality and therefore cannot be regarded as disclosing that reality in its full concreteness. Two assumptions lay behind this empiricism; first, it was taken to be certain that whereas we may be mistaken about the existence and the nature of the object before us, we cannot be mistaken about our *perception* at least of the nature of the object, because what is immediately present to the mind, i.e., our perception, is beyond all doubt. Second, since the conditions of sense perception are said to vary so that, for example, if I place one hand in a pail of water and my hand feels warm and then place the other hand in the same water and my hand feels cold, it was concluded that since the water itself cannot be both hot and cold, I must not be experiencing the water at all, but rather, the feelings in my own hand. The upshot of these two assumptions was that experience came to be seen as something cut off from objective reality; experience took on the status of a private veil or screen, certain within itself but devoid of any guarantee that it is experience of anything beyond itself. On this view of the matter, experience, instead of disclosing what there is, actually encloses itself within a circle of privacy.

It would be a great mistake to suppose that the foregoing discussion is merely speculative and has no direct bearing on the main theme. It should be obvious that if the foregoing view of experience is correct, it would be quite futile to speak of experiencing God and equally futile to think of any experience signaling the presence of a transforming spirit. The most that could be said is that a given person has had or reported the occurrence of such and such feelings—a feeling of joy, of peace, of forgiveness, or of acceptance, for example; but that these feelings point beyond themselves to a transcendent reality or that they are experiences in which such a reality is ingredient cannot be said. In view of the closeness of religion to experience, any view of experience that reduces it to irrelevance or renders it unavailable for the expression of religious insight must on that account alone be seriously called into question. And, indeed, this view was called into question by the proponents of American pragmatism and radical empiricism.

Pragmatists and radical empiricists sought a return to actual experiencing in its many dimensions for clues to the discovery of what experience *is* like; they did not remain satisfied with a theory of what experience *must be* like if it is to make knowledge possible or solve the problem of error. Two considerations stand out as essential. According to what I have called the reconstructed view of experience, there is no need whatever to suppose that we do not experience or encounter realities themselves, but only our own perceptions, for in fact this subjectivist supposition is itself part of a theory for explaining error and cannot be regarded as an incorrigible intuition of what happens. Reality is open to experience, and man is open to reality; experience, though it is always realized by someone, somewhere and somewhen, is not a private set of mental representatives or copies of what is encountered. Experience is, instead, an intersubjective way of meeting reality which issues in the funded result of many encounters whereby it is disclosed. That funded result in the form of qualities, relations, events, objects, purposes, meanings is a genuine disclosure of the real world. As such, this result is far richer and more complex than the impressions, representations and sensory data envisaged by classical empiricism. Moreover, it is not confined to "consciousness" as a theater of privacy standing in contrast to the objective world. Reference to intersubjectivity serves to focus the second consideration mentioned; our experience has a shared character which gives to it an objective or public form reaching beyond the limits of what is encountered by any one individual. This public form is both the presupposition and the outcome of our common life and its communities. Two persons, for example, are able to share their experiences and witness to their mutual understanding because they start with the belief that experience is continuous. And wherever they are mistaken in this belief, that fact itself can be discovered only by continuing the process of sharing and comparing reports of what we have encountered. In short, experience takes on an objective form as custom, tradition and habitual life which serve as the basis of all human community. Nowhere is this truth better illustrated than in the religious community itself. The experience of a Job in despair over his own suffering in the face of his faith, or the experience of a Paul expressing the power of the love which, in his belief, never fails, is not to be confined to these individuals alone nor to the limits of their individuated consciousness. These experiences disclose structures of human existence, structures of life in the world, structures of love and despair as man experiences them. Countless individuals over the centuries have *shared* similar experiences; giving vivid testimony to their intersubjective and pervasive character. And there need be no conflict between experience disclosing an objective structure and being realized in individual lives where it has a unique meaning. Experience can be both pervasive and unique. The decisive import which experience has for the life of a person can be seen in the impact made by what I shall call, following Dewey, *an* experience.

We often speak of experience as if it were an uninterrupted flow of events with contemporaneous fields of content, but this conception is apt to be misleading unless we stress the fact that experience is punctuated and includes, in the good figure of James, perching places as well as flight. Experience is realized for each of us in *experiences* or situations having a certain unity marked out be a definite beginning and a terminus or closure, and characterized by a quality which enables us to identify them as individual experiences. Illustrations abound and they are familiar. We may recall *that* terrifying experience when we nearly drowned; or *that* sublime experience of natural beauty when we first saw the Victoria Falls; or again we may dwell on *that* disappointing experience when someone we depended on for help failed to come to our assistance. Each instance represents a determinate, individual experience carved out, so to speak, from the stream of ongoing events and each is identified by some dominant quality which may be called its upshot or import and which has impressed us because of its peculiar significance for our life. *An* experience represents the apex of meaningfulness and importance in a course of life; such experiences frequently carry with them a purpose and an orientation which give point to our life as a whole.

Among experiences of this sort we must include those that have decisive or religious import because they involve either the encounter with the Holy, or some awe-inspiring and arresting confrontation that is an occasion when something is disclosed to us concerning the quality of our life as a totality. The experience reported by Isaiah in the 6th chapter of the book of Isaiah furnishes an excellent example. It is a unified whole, *an* experience, and a sequence of insights as well. To begin with, it is identified by date: "In the year King Uzziah died . . ." and the memorable event is the encounter with the Holy One of Israel: "I saw the Lord. . . ." The vision leads at once to the critical awareness of the gulf between that Holiness and man's existence: "I am undone, I am a man of unclean lips and I dwell in the midst of a people of unclean lips." And that is not all; the experience is more than an occasion for contemplation as if it were esthetic and not essentially religious and moral. There follows the demand for a response, a call to action; and "there came a voice saying, 'Whom shall I send? Who will go for us?' " Isaiah answers: "Here am I. Send me." Isaiah ever afterward regarded that experience as decisive; it was his call to the prophetic office.

Paul's experience on the Damascus road is another case in point. Paul had many powerful and memorable experiences, but none was to outrank this one in importance because it involved the basic orientation of his life and being. Here was an experience which disclosed to him the purpose behind all of his experiences. It is as if the ground upon which he had been standing, the ground from which he persecuted the adherents of the new faith, was suddenly revealed to him in its truth, and set in contrast to a new ground which was to be the ground of a new person. Paul ever afterward regarded that experience as decisive; it was the event of his transformation, and witnesses to the power of *an* experience in human life.

Enough has been said *about* understanding and experience in relation to faith; ultimately everything depends on what Hegel called "working the matter out," which means executing the program in detail. In short, we must show how the experiential appeal actually leads to understanding or helps us to apprehend the content of faith. Hence, in the succeeding chapters I shall attempt to show how the presentation of analogues in experience brings us to an understanding of man, of God, of Christ and of the church or community of love founded by the One who first brought it into being. Naturally, such an ambitious program cannot be fully realized here, but something can be done to show how the analogy of experience may serve us in a contemporary quest of "faith seeking understanding." Though theology has traditionally begun with God as its primary point of reference, the experiential approach requires that we begin instead with man or the being who asks the question about God. Therefore, I start with man and what I call his "circular predicament" and then proceed to an understanding of God as the transcendent center of intention, passing on to Christ as the concrete manifestation of that center, ending with the community of love (the Beloved Community) as the locus of transforming power in history which holds out the promise of escape from man's predicament.

III

Analogy and Experience

The resort to analogy in religious thought and discourse is dictated in the first instance by the obvious fact that while our experience of the world, ourselves and others is accessible and mediated through sensible things, no corresponding sensible apprehension of God is open to us. No one "sees" God in the sense in which he "sees" his house or his neighbor. The Judeo-Christian tradition has always insisted on the necessity of mediation, not only with respect to the mediate disclosure of God in Christ, but also in the form of signs and symbols throughout the universe pointing beyond themselves to the divine. "No man hath seen God at any time" is a recurrent biblical theme. The aim is to speak of a reality which is not a sensible object among others, and yet it is not possible to do so without recourse to the finite and conditioned experience which we have. To speak of God as love or as loving, it is necessary to have some understanding of what love means in man's experience. And even if it is claimed that we have been given a direct revelation of what love means with respect to God, we would still have to *understand* that disclosure by recourse to love as it exists between human beings.

The mark of man's finitude is that he is forced to speak about God and his relations to man and the universe in terms of similarity and analogy. The classical doctrine of analogy was intended to clarify the relation between what is said about God and what is said about man and the world. That doctrine was an attempt to mark out a third alternative between two extremes, each of which was regarded as unsatisfactory. At one extreme stood the view that the term "love" when applied to God is absolutely discontinuous in meaning with the same term as applied to man. On this view, to say that "God loves" and to say that "man loves" is to use the same term "equivocally," which is to say that there is not one but two terms and absolutely no overlap of meaning. The consequence is either that we can say nothing whatever about God, or nothing which is to be understood by recourse to a meaning dependent on human experience. At the other extreme stood the view that only one term is involved and it is used "univocally" so that when we say "God loves" and "man loves" the term "love" is meant in exactly the same sense in both cases. The difficulty, of course, with this view is that either God's love is reduced to the finite level and the divine otherness is obscured, or man's love is divinized by becoming identical with the love of God. This latter consequence has not always been noticed because of the common tendency to suppose that the only love in question is the love available in man's experience. In either case, however, the otherness between man and God is canceled and this is a consequence which cannot be accepted by faith.

The appeal to analogy is, therefore, an attempt to find a position between the two extremes; in speaking about God and man the term "love" is to be used neither in two absolutely different senses nor in one exactly identical sense, but in an analogical sense, which is to say that one love is *similar* to the other, where "similar" means neither "absolutely different" nor "absolutely identical." To be similar is therefore to combine sameness and otherness, continuity and discontinuity in a peculiar way. The relationship of similarity involved in religious expressions cannot be determined in a quantitative way as if we could say that the love which is God's is identical with human love in X number of respects and different from it in Y number of respects. The similar is a qualitatively distinct relationship standing between the two extreme cases of identity and absolute otherness in precisely the manner in which Aristotle's mean states were determined as qualitatively distinct. Courage stands between cowardice and rashness, but it cannot be derived from either by quantitative adjustments; courage is not cowardice strengthened by a large dose of rashness, nor is it rashness tempered with the right amount of cowardice. And yet all three dispositions cohere in the same universe of discourse because each is directed to the same situation, a challenge which a person must meet either in judgment, in overt action, or in both.

What similarity means when we attempt to use experience itself as the medium for understanding religious insight needs to be further clarified, but first it is essential to attempt to clear up a widespread confusion that exists concerning the supposedly peculiar character of religious thought and discourse. There is a natural tendency to suppose that ordinary experience and the knowledge based upon it are couched in terms that are wholly "literal" and validly reflective of reality, whereas all expressions of the religious concsiousness are "symbolic" in a sense supposed to deprive them of either a proper referent or a clear meaning. The dyadic distinction between literal and symbolic, in addition to standing in need of further clarification itself, fails to do justice to the character of religious expressions. To begin with, the distinction oversimplifies the actual situation by describing all of the experience and knowledge in which religious considerations play little or no part as "literal" or mirrorlike reflections of what is, while at the same time excluding religious expressions from this category. But if at least one of the lessons to be learned from the contemporary analysis of language is to be taken seriously, it should be clear that this so-called literal domain is a myth. The fact is that a spectrum of related but not identical meanings develops in the use of every term within the supposed literal domain itself. Consider, for example, the spectrum of meaning attaching to so simple a term as "in" when it is used in the following ways. "I put the key *in* the lock"; "What idea do you have *in* mind?" "He does not have his heart *in* his work." "I have a considerable investment *in* that enterprise." It seems clear enough that while each use of the term "in" coheres with the others by contrast with the antonym "out," we cannot claim that the term is used in exactly the same sense in all the instances. I do not have an idea "in" my mind in the same sense as the key is "in" the lock, nor does anyone have his heart "in" his work in either of these senses.

Suppose we now ask: Which of the several senses of the term "in" represents the "literal" sense such that in relation to it the others are to be judged "symbolic" or "metaphorical"? There seems to be no obvious answer to the question unless we select the abstract spatial connotation of the term "the key is *in* the lock" as providing us with a paradigm or "core" meaning which in turn gives us some insight into the other uses. This selective operation is in fact the procedure we invariably follow; there need be no objection to it in principle if two conditions are observed. First, the priority attached to the core meaning, in this case the spatial meaning, or the relation of containing and being contained in, must be seen as derivative from familiar, direct experiences[1] that are easily grasped, and such priority must not be attributed to the superior status of mathematics or to the supposed "objectivity" of space as a category determining reality. Second, it is not to be supposed that uses of the term not identical with the core meaning are on that account to be denied either meaning or validity.

The essential point is that the distinction between "literal" and "symbolic," often regarded as clear and absolute, is in fact a relative one, thoroughly dependent on the fact that a spectrum of meanings for a given term invariably breaks out within the domain of the so-called "literal" itself. The crucial consequence of this fact for the philosophy of religion is that the transposition of terms whose meaning is based on sensible experience to the transcendent referent of religious expressions does *not* represent some special and thought-defying case, but is instead one more instance of a phenomenon to be found in every use of language. Ludwig Wittgenstein has given clear and convincing examples of the use of the same term in different contexts such that the term has neither the same meaning in each occurrence nor an entirely different meaning. In the above example, the various uses of the

---

1. The fact that the *concept* of space is basic to abstract, theoretical sciences does not preclude our direct apprehension of spatial relations in many ordinary situations.

term "in" do not express a purely univocal meaning and yet they are not entirely equivocal because they do cohere around the core meaning of containing and being contained as opposed to excluding and being excluded. And it is the existence of the core meaning as derivative from direct experience which provides a basis for using that experience in an analogical way.

Discussions, both classical and modern, of analogy as the characteristic form of religious expressions have invariably focused on predication and the meaning of terms, an emphasis which has been enhanced in recent discussion by the widespread concern among philosophers for language and its structures. There is no doubt that this emphasis has contributed much to the proper understanding of religious discourse, but it remains abstract, nevertheless, because it directs attention primarily to the syntax and semantics of expression and away from the richness of experience which the language is supposed to express. The importance for religion of the emphasis on experience itself and not only on its expression has not always been noticed. Religion is through and through an experiential affair in the sense that it concerns the interpretation in the ultimate dimension of what an individual person actually undergoes and suffers and which is in fact the substance of his life. It is one thing for a person to entertain religious concepts and doctrines and to learn that they are interpreted in a certain way for all members of a religious community, but it is quite another for a person to come to the realization that it is his own life and experience which are thus interpreted. The central fact is that the individual is actually participating in the experience through which the understanding of religious insight is attained. Language will, of course, be involved, but exclusive concentration on language and its rules could obscure the fact that it is the experiencing itself which is the substance of both life and religion. It is for this reason that I proposed to speak of an *analogy of experience* where a person's own experience is brought into play as the medium through which its religious meaning is to be understood. The task is to explain how experience can function in this way and what grounds can be offered for its analogical use.

The first point to be noticed is that whenever an analogy, a similitude or a model is employed for the purpose of gaining understanding, an explicit asymmetry is involved. That is to say, there is presupposed at the outset a distinction between something *to be understood* or made intelligible and something *by means of which* this understanding is to be accomplished. And in the nature of the case it is taken for granted that the latter is more accessible in experience or better understood than the former. It is also assumed that the converse of this relationship does not hold; if I seek to understand X through analogy with Y, it is not supposed that I am explicitly attempting to understand Y through analogy with X. The actual comparison may indeed lead to an apprehension of details about Y which had previously gone unnoticed and these may prove to be of further significance in the understanding of X, but this does not alter the fact that the original purpose of the analogy was to understand X in terms of Y and not conversely.

Since there is considerable use made of analogies and models in scientific thought, two illustrations will serve to make clear what is meant by the asymmetry just mentioned. Analogies are appealed to in science both for the interpretation of terms and as a means of understanding a particular theory. Clerk Maxwell sought to interpret the concept of the self-diffusion of molecules in a gas by appealing to an analogy between the behavior of the molecules and that of bees in a swarm. He wrote:

If we wish to form a representation of what is going on among the molecules in calm air, we cannot do better than observe a swarm of bees, when every individual bee is flying furiously, first in one direction and then in another, while the swarm as a whole either remains at rest, or sails slowly through the air.[2]

In the above case it seems quite clear that the behavior of the bees is regarded as accessible and open to observation and that this observation is to provide us with insight into the behavior of the molecules, which is not accessible in the same way. It would be

2. The passage is found in James Clerk Maxwell, *Scientific Papers*, W.D. Niven, ed. (New York, 1965) II, p. 368. I am indebted to Peter Achinstein's *Concepts of Science* (Baltimore, 1968) for this reference.

quite absurd to suggest that the relationship is symmetrical and that we are attempting to form a representation of the behavior of the bees in terms of the behavior of the molecules. The presupposition of the analogy is that the logical direction of thought runs from the more open and transparent experience to the less, and not conversely. It may indeed happen that there is some feature of the molecule mass which we can determine—perhaps its relative density—and go on to ask whether the swarm of bees is such that it makes sense to speak of its relative density. But I believe it would be admitted that it is the bees which are directly open to observation and that it seems an unnecessary complication to attempt to understand them and their behavior by appealing to the behavior of the molecules which is clearly less understood.

Another and similar example is found in the development of the theory of light. In proposing a wave theory as opposed to the corpuscular theory of Newton, the seventeenth-century scientist Huygens wrote the following with regard to both light and sound: "I call them [light and sound] waves from their resemblance to those which are seen to be formed in water when a stone is thrown into it, and which present a successive spreading as circles, though these arise from another cause, and are only in a flat surface."[3] Once again, the presupposition of such an analogy is that the behavior of a body of water when a stone is thrown into it is open to observation and well known so that it can form the basis for an understanding of both light and sound as essentially wavelike phenomena. The analogy would furnish no insight unless this presupposition were sound; otherwise we would be attempting to explain the obscure by the even more obscure.

The use of analogies drawn from accessible experience for the understanding of religious insight, while not identical with the use of analogies in scientific inquiry, involves the same asymmetry to be found in the foregoing illustrations. In attempting to understand what could be meant by divine love or by atonement,

3. Christaan Huygens, *Treatise on Light* (Chicago, 1945), p. 4.

we must use as a base the appropriate human experience which is open to us, always mindful of the fact that the object of our inquiry is to gain insight into realities transcending our experience. Even if we suppose that the experience of God realized in the lives of Moses and the prophets, or the atonement manifested in Christ, represent the paradigm cases to be understood, the approach to that understanding must be through the experience open to us. These paradigm cases, to be sure, go beyond, and are not exhausted by, what can be understood by analogy from human experience, but it is precisely this "beyond" which demands the use of analogy in the first instance. Were a clear and direct insight into the meaning of the paradigm cases available to us, there would be no need to proceed by a circuitous route. But such an insight is not available and the entire biblical tradition testifies against its possibility for finite beings. God is invariably represented as made manifest in and through another; this fact is at the same time the principal reason why analogies and similitudes are necessary.

A further consequence of the asymmetrical character of all analogies whether in science or religion is that whatever we are trying to understand in terms of experience that is more familiar to us is not exhaustively known or understood by any given analogy. For the fact that it is necessary to resort to an analogy shows that the object or concept we are trying to understand does not belong to available and familiar experience. That the more transparent experience, however, does not exhaust the nature and the meaning of what is being understood through it follows from the fact that the one is only similar to, and not identical with, the other, and from the logical consideration that it is impossible to support the claim with respect to a particular analogy that *every* feature to be understood in the problematic object or concept is represented in that analogy. To return to the examples cited, the behavior of the molecules in the gas is said to be no more than similar to the behavior of the bees in the swarm, and beyond the reference to the darting back and forth of individual bees and the stationary position or general drift of the swarm, there is no claim that the molecules behave in no other ways than those specified in the analogy. Other properties and behavioral patterns may require additional analogies. The case is the same for analogies in religion. When it is said that the divine forgiveness is similar to that of human forgiveness what is meant is that in both cases there is a misdeed followed by repentance where the injured party accepts that repentance and the person, thus transcending the justice of retaliation. But there is no claim that what transpires on the human plane exhausts the meaning of divine forgiveness, because there are always imperfections in human forgiveness—that no finite being can in fact be free of an element of vengeance in his motive—which cannot be attributed to the divine.

The human limitation implied in our being forced to resort to analogies serves as a constant reminder that these analogies are not more than analogies and consequently that they never exhaust the meaning of the experiences and concepts ingredient in the normative disclosure of God for the Judeo-Christian tradition. We still see through a "glass darkly" though we are not entirely in the dark.

The proposal to employ experience as the basis for analogy in the religious sphere has two aspects; on the one hand, it means the appeal to specific experiences as a way of understanding religious concepts. On the other hand, it means an ontological claim concerning the status and function of experience as such, namely, that it is capable of serving as a medium of interpretation between the finite world and its ultimate ground. In some naturalistic and materialist positions, experience is viewed, in the figure introduced by Santayana, as a brief flash of light, an evanescent source of illumination, in the midst of a vast ocean of "objective" reality which is just there in an opaque darkness. The truth which such an outlook misses entirely is that experience as meaningful content expressible in a mobile language is itself a reality that is realized only as the consequence of a peculiar attunement between man as a sign-using animal and the intelligible structures of things. The prejudice according to which man's experience is an epiphenomenal duplicate of what there is, a sort of private showing on an interior, mental screen of all the things in the world, must be overcome. Experience is an identifiable emergent in the linear sequence of an evolutionary process, and as such it forms the medium through which the structures and the significances of things are realized and brought to critical expression. Until this basic fact about experience is understood, it will continue to be excluded from the real world—the world of facts, of objects, or events and processes—and its function as the interpreter of the world's meaning will be lost. Experience has a valid status in being, and any ontology which deprives it of such status is on that account erroneous.

The justification of analogy in religion, the warrant for holding that analogies of experience are valid means for rendering religious insight intelligible, must rest with the ontological claim. A particular analogy drawn from experience, such as the use of the tale concerning Joseph and his brothers for understanding the concept of atonement, may be more or less adequate for the elucidation of a given concept or doctrine, but every such analogy depends ultimately on the validity of the analogical use of experience as such, which is precisely why a general theory is called for. The problem may be stated thus: if religious insight is to be made intelligible, and if such insight into the meaning of existence as a whole for finite beings cannot be a matter of immediate or intuitive apprehension, the question arises as to what feature of existence is able to perform the mediating function. Transposing the question into logical terms, it is seen as a form of the problem of self-representation: given a whole of reality, to what extent can one of its proper parts serve to express or interpret the meaning of that whole? When stated thus in general and abstract terms, the question will be seen at once as too comprehensive for the purposes of the philosophy of religion. For here we are not attempting to set forth a general ontology, but seeking instead for an ontological basis upon which the understanding of religious insight can be made to depend.

The proposal, illustrated in what follows, for an analogy of experience, is to be understood as asserting that human experience is the "proper part" in existence which has the capacity to represent and interpret the meaning of the religious ideas which in turn purport to express the meaning of existence from the religious point of view. Despite all that has been said about God's being "wholly other" and "hidden" from the revelatory standpoint, the fact remains that these determinations themselves represent interpretations of a revealed content, and to understand them we must have recourse to our own experience of what it means to be *not* "wholly other" or "hidden." As Berdyaev pointed out long ago, those who seek to preserve the "mystery" of God against the impious encroachments of philosophical theologians have already overstepped the boundary they would themselves enforce. For to invoke the category of mystery is to invite the question, What is a mystery? and we must then appeal to our own experience of what cannot properly be called a mystery in order to understand what we are talking about. The task is not that of dissolving the mystery, but of understanding what we are saying of God when we refer to him in this way. Let God be as "wholly other" as anyone could wish, the reception, understanding and appropriation of this "other" cannot be realized without recourse to human experience. The supposition that such recourse "subjectivizes" God, or reduces God to purely human terms is simply unfounded, as unfounded as the same supposition would be in the case of finite objects and persons. Neither the table nor my neighbor is reduced to some subjective form of existence as the result of being experienced by me. The equation of experience with the private, the "mental" and the subjective is an error stemming from the false conception of experience handed down to us by the classical British empiricsts. It has been the lasting contribution of both pragmatism and radical empiricism to expose that error.

Experience is a unique level in reality and it serves as a vantage point for the interpretation of the whole of existence. If this vantage point is a reliable medium for the disclosure of the natural world in the sciences, there is no reason why it should not also be a means to the understanding of the content of faith. Should it be objected that, since God is "wholly other," human experience is worthless as a medium of understanding, the reply is that for the Judeo-Christian tradition God can never be understood in a sense that makes impossible his ingredience in man's historical experience, or, even more crucially, in a human life. It is difficult to understand how those who claim to adopt an incarnational basis for theology can continue to proclaim that God is in all respects "wholly other" than the human life and experience that were made to serve as the divine embodiment. The same difficulty appears if one considers the relation from the other side; if God is in all respects "wholly other" than man, how would he understand man and his experience? The process philosophers and theologians have seen this problem very clearly when they point out that man has finite and contingent knowledge of himself and, since God cannot know *less* than man does, God must understand this finite knowledge which man has of himself. In order for God to encompass himself and comprehend man at the same time, he cannot be in all respects "wholy other" than man and his experience.

To return to the use of analogies of experience in the understanding of faith, it is essential to lay down two basic conditions which serve to distinguish the use of a term or experience in relation to God from the corresponding use in relation to man. First, the nature of the being characterized determines the mode in which the characteristic exists or is manifested. Second, since God transcends and includes man and all finite being (and never conversely) the meaning of any term or experience used to make intelligible an insight of faith about God must be *at least* as rich as the meaning which the term or experience has for human beings. With regard to the first, the divine love characterizes God's being—God *is* love—and thus differs in important respects from every instance of human love; man "has" love, but he is not love, and hence love is never wholly constitutive of his being, even if he has love to an unusual degree. Moreover, the love of God intending the forgiveness of a person who repents of his folly stands related to a divine knowledge which has the special character of including a *conspectus* of the life pattern of the individual intended insofar as it has been realized. Therefore, for the divine knowledge, the act of forgiveness stands related to an understanding of the total personality. In the case of one person forgiving another, the intention to forgive stands related to what is never more than a fragmentary and frequently erroneous knowledge of the other person. The same contrast is manifested in the case of an intention to perform some act or service which is to contribute to another's welfare. With respect to God, such an intention is related to a conspectus of the individual's life in its totality as so far realized in time, and the benevolent deed would be informed by a knowledge of what in fact would contribute to his welfare, whereas in the relations between man and man the intention to benefit another is limited by its relation to an imperfect and fragmentary knowledge of the one whose life we would enhance.

The difference between human and divine knowledge is, of course, not the only difference to be noted; differences in will and intention are also involved. When I attempt to act justly toward another man, I do so always as a finite being to whom justice also needs to be done. Therefore, my action is never "disinterested" and is always tainted with the possibility of ulterior motives at work. God's action, on the other hand, is not infected by this limitation since he stands beyond the need to demand for himself the justice which I, as finite being, can never avoid trying to exact from my fellow beings. It is for this reason that God can in fact act justly whereas no finite being can ever do so.

Are we then to say that the love, the benevolent intention and the justice are absolutely different in the two cases? I believe not, and the chief reason is that we understand and judge the *imperfection* of human love and justice by comparison with the divine for whom those limitations are transcended. It would make no sense to pronounce human purposes and motives imperfect according to the divine standard, as in fact the entire biblical tradition does, if the human and the divine were completely discontinuous with each other. The use of analogy from experience for understanding faith does not mean that God's nature is identical with the human experience used analogically, but rather, that God's nature is not entirely different from what we can understand through that experience.

The fact that the use of analogy in the sphere of religious

meaning represents an indirect mode of approach has frequently led to the question of its justification. There need be no objection to the raising of this question, but it is essential to be clear about exactly what is involved in the call for justification. We cannot reasonably ask for a form of proof or verification for analogies which, were it forthcoming, would render the appeal to analogy unnecessary in the first instance. It is, however, possible to furnish indirect support for the reliability of experience as an analogical medium as long as it is understood that this support is not intended to transform analogy into something that is expendable.[4]

Argumentations are available for showing that experience is a reliable medium for the disclosure of the real. There is no way of showing with respect to a given analogy, that between our experience of forgiving another person and the forgiveness of God, for example, that it carries with it proof or justification of the reality of a divine forgiveness. But there is available indirect support for the belief that experience as such is a legitimate medium for analogy enabling us to gain some understanding of faith. Three lines of argument may be cited.

First, experience is an identifiable emergent in the evolution-

4. A clear and consistent logical model of "indirect support" has been provided by C.S. Peirce in his paper, "A Neglected Argument for the Reality of God." After distinguishing between an "argument" as any form of reasoning leading to a definite belief, and an "argumentation" as a form of reasoning based on explicitly formulated premises, he set forth the hypothesis of God's reality as the result of an "argument" based on musement and the perception of the need to find a coordinator of the three universes of experience (Ideas, Brute Actualities and Signs). His "humble argument," as he called it, is not itself a strict proof or argumentation, but the result of an experiential situation in which the hypothesis of God, vague and indeterminate, is forced upon our consciousness as an item of belief. He does not, however, leave the matter there, but goes on to furnish an argumentation based on an analysis of man's capacity to frame relevant and testable hypotheses and the consequent need to assume some form of "attunement" between the human mind and the intelligible structures of things. The crucial point is that this argumentation is *not* meant to replace the "humble argument," but rather, to provide it with indirect support by showing that the power to frame hypotheses exhibited in it is generally trustworthy. The upshot is that Peirce's model does not contain an argumentation for God's reality, but an argument which is said to be reliable in itself because of the grounds furnished by the argumentation indirectly supporting it.

ary history of man and human consciousness and thus possesses a legitimate status in the scheme of things. Far from being an evanescent, "mental" addition to an otherwise fixed or finished reality, experience represents the result or realization of certain necessary conditions in the cosmic process. Without the existence of a sign-using animal, on the one hand, and a world exhibiting a degree of order sufficient to allow for recurrence of form and pattern, on the other, no such reality as human experience could have made its appearance. That experience has the status of an objective constituent of reality—*not* the constituter of reality—becomes manifest when we consider that it represents the result of the intelligible togetherness of what is expressible in nature and the capacity of the sign-using animal to express. Experience makes its appearance at the intersection of man and whatever there is to encounter, to explain and to interpret. The tendency to enclose experience entirely within man as something existent only within the inner recess of consciousness causes us to lose sight of its peculiar character as an emergent reality conditioned as much by the surrounding universe to be encountered as by the one who encounters. To appeal to experience, therefore, as a medium through which to understand religious insight is to appeal to a reality which has roots in the entire cosmic process; it is not an appeal merely to man's mind or consciousness as entities sealed off from the rest of things. If experience is the medium through which the world becomes meaningful to man, there is no reason why it should not serve as a channel for the understanding of religious truth.

Second, experience is pervasive and is capable of assuming intersubjective form. Intersubjectivity is a determinate characteristic of experience and it can be reached in at least three ways; experimental intervention and control, the constant reaffirmation of the pervasive in experience through the critical consciousness of a historical community, and the comparison of experience across cultural boundaries. The obvious success of the various sciences in attaining intersubjective results is a function of man's capacity to isolate systems and to institute in them processes of change under controlled conditions which are public in the sense that they are, in principle, reproducible. Insofar as scientific investigation is carried out within a community of inquirers each of whom acknowledges and is willing to be bound by the conditions for objective inquiry, the resulting opinions take on intersubjective character.

Experience and experiment, however, are not synonymous and it is simply not the case that all phenomena in human experience can become the object of experimental inquiry. There are, however, other paths to intersubjectivity. The experience upon which religion is based and which religious insight seeks to interpret assumes a public and intersubjective form as the tradition definitive of a historical community which endures. A community exists in and through the medium of shared experience, and it is precisely through sharing that the pervasive in experience is discovered and set apart from all that is purely idiosyncratic or confined to the isolated individual. The history of religion is rich in illustrations of the power of shared experience; the prophet or reformer who seeks to transform or reform his tradition on the basis of insights which he alone has will be successful only to the extent that his new truth expresses what is pervasive in the experience of all members of the community. When a Luther, for example, appeals to the role of individual conscience in determining religious faith, his appeal will not be understood at the outset nor will it come to be incorporated into the life of the community unless the experience to which he points *is recognizable by others as forming a part of what they also suffer and undergo.* The false prophet is false in large measure because what he declares to be so fails to be corroborated by the experience of the community to which he speaks and his proposed truth comes to be revealed as the expression of a willful and wayward spirit. The discovery of the pervasive and the intersubjective structures of experience is possible through the life of an ongoing community in which experience can be shared and compared. This discovery, like that which characterizes the outcome of the experimental sciences, takes time to achieve and, when attained, it represents a funded product, a convergence of outlook which unifies many diverse individuals. There are in fact instructive parallels between the working of the scientific community in reaching a generally accepted opinion and the manner in which religious communities succeed in separating what is perennial in experience from what is merely private or parochial.

The third path to intersubjectivity in experience is an extension of the second and it is more difficult to follow because it leads beyond the boundaries of any one religious community or tradition. The aim is to discover through a comparative method the homogeneities and heterogeneities in experience across traditions, religious, cultural and ethnic. When does there exist an identity of experience realized which goes unheeded because no attempt has been made to go beyond and beneath the differing languages in which such experience has found expression? There is, for example, a deep, though abstract, continuity of experience to be found at the roots of every major enduring religion. That continuity is illustrated in the recurrence of what we may call the *diagnosis of the human predicament* in the light of some conception of what man's life in its ideal or essential fulfillment would be like. The pervasive experience is that man historically exhibits some basic flaw or defect which stands in the way of his realization. The diagnosis of this defect, to be sure, is not the same in every religious tradition, but the recurrence of the pattern of diagnosis remains. The Buddha, for example, as a result of his Enlightenment, found the root of human suffering in man's failure to shape and limit the natural boundlessness of his desire and in his tendency to attach himself to what is illusory and evanescent in existence. Christianity, on the other hand, in accordance with the vision of God as creator, has traced the flaw in man to the recalcitrance of his will and his refusal to accept the fact of his being a creature. The conceptions of the flaw differs as between the two traditions, but the pattern of experiencing and diagnosing a flaw remains.

In addition to such structural recurrence in experience, there may well exist other patterns of continuity to be discovered through the process of comparison. To what extent, for example, is the experience of "effortless striving" so much emphasized in the Taoist tradition and in other Oriental religions, continuous with the experience of "grace" in Western religion? In both cases there is a strong sense that the beatitude to be attained is not simply within the grasp of human effort and that as such it cannot be "willed" into existence. Or again, to what extent is there continuity between the Buddhist experience of "emptying" the self of all illusory thoughts concerning its uniqueness and substantiality, and the Christian experience of standing "naked" before God without any claim on the divine mercy based on righteousness or merit? These questions cannot, of course, be answered here; they are meant, however, to point to the possibility of intersubjectivity and continuity in experience at points where such features might not be thought to exist.

The foregoing considerations all point in the direction of providing grounds for believing in the intersubjectivity of experience and thus give indirect support to the thesis that experience as such is a trustworthy medium for the understanding of religious insight.

IV

Man and the Circular Predicament

Alexander Pope laid hold of something basic in our modern consciousness when he wrote that oft-quoted couplet, "'Tis not for us the ways of God to scan; the proper study of mankind is man." Skepticism and uncertainty about God have made themselves felt among us for almost two centuries and may be said to have reached a high point in our time, but the problem of man, his nature and destiny, persists. Our perplexity about ourselves is hardly less great than our bewilderment concerning what we are to understand about God in an age when, for some at any rate, God has died. A focal point in Christian faith is its understanding of man and its diagnosis of the human predicament. At no other point do we find so clearly outlined what I call the negative judgment on existence which is at the root of the religious consciousness. Popular conceptions of religion, including those of Christian faith as well, invariably identify religion with "values" or "ideals" and it is supposed that whereas the actual state of the world manifests evil, suffering and injustice, the standpoint of faith requires us to ignore this actual world and shows us that there is another world in which the distortions of the present one do not exist. In short, religion is often viewed as romantic self-deception, a stance which does not dare to begin with the facts of existence, but must abscond to a transcendent realm in which all is neat and tidy. Such a view is as erroneous as it is widespread.

One of the most striking facts about the outlook not only of Christianity, but of Buddhism and some forms of the Hindu tradition as well, is a profound sense that human existence is infected with some basic flaw, some form of distortion, which stands in vivid contrast to what existence might be, what it should be, what it was meant to be. The basic insight of these three traditions—Christianity, Buddhism and Hinduism—different as they are in certain other crucial respects, converges in a realistic appraisal of natural existence. They all insist that existence is in some fundamental way *separated from* its true nature and being. The common message is that both man and the world are "seriously out of joint," and that man's goal is something which all are in danger of missing because of some actual flaw or defect determining our being. This critical and negative judgment on existence centers on man and points to what I shall call a diagnosis of the human predicament. The key to understanding the content of any faith is found in discovering exactly how it proposes to diagnose this predicament: What factor or factors in existence are believed to separate man from his true being, what is the nature of that being and how is the flaw that separates us from it to be overcome? If we are to have any understanding of what redemption means, or what it means to be made whole again, we must also have some understanding of the broken situation in which we exist and from which we are to be redeemed. And one of the cardinal reasons why so many at present find little meaning in the ideas of redemption and reconciliation is that a vivid sense of the distortion of existence has been lost. Such was the state of those referred to in the New Testament who saw no need of a physician. When this happens or when the distortion in human existence does find acknowledgment but is looked upon merely as something accidental or evanescent to be overcome in terms of human ingenuity, the idea that a redemption is needed sounds strange. On the other hand, it would be folly to deny that presenting the idea of man's predicament solely in the language of the traditional "drama of salvation" would make it sound equally strange in a world where the languages of technology, of economics, of the social sciences and of politics virtually determine our consciousness. My aim, however, is not an excursion into comparative religion, but an analysis of Christian faith seeking understanding. The characteristic concept in the Christian diagnosis of the human predicament is the concept of sin. Sin in the traditional understanding points to the flaw in the being of the natural man which separates him from God. The task is to see what this means in experiential terms so that it can be recognized in the pattern of human life surrounding us. There are, to be sure, many problems connected with man's separation from God or the ground of his existence which are beyond our scope. My chief concern is to concentrate on the pervasive structural idea of a human predicament as such, in order to come to some understanding of how it is conceived specifically in Christian perspective.

Too often the idea of man's separation or estrangement from God has been understood exclusively in terms of specific deeds that are declared contrary either to some version of the divine law or to derived readings of that law expressed in social customs and conventions. This way of approach is too narrow and misses a fundamental feature of the situation. Specific sins or "missings of the mark" there are, to be sure, but they alone are not adequate for expressing what is meant by man's estrangement. For there is not only the *doing* dimension of human existence manifest in identifiable actions and their character, but there is also the *being* dimension that points to the quality of a form of life taken as a whole. The difference may be expressed in terms of the important but not always appreciated distinction between the *religious* and the *moral.* The former concerns the being, the ultimate orientation of the self, the focus of unconditional devotion, while the latter has to do with the actions one should perform in relation to the beings in the world. The religious points to the question: What am I to be? and the moral to the question: What am I to do? The two dimensions are set in dramatic relation to each other by the writer of the First Epistle of John, "If a man say, I love God, and hates his brother, he is a liar" (4:20). Two points are noteworthy here; first, the dimensions are distinguished and not identified, and second, the two are so related that the religious relationship demands a certain kind of action in the moral sphere and if such action does not follow, the validity of the original religious relationship is called into question. If, in other words, the person exists in a state of estrangement or separation from God, his conduct will show the marks of that separation. But the religious and the moral are not to be confused; estrangement as a state refers to man's *being*, while his consequent failures in the moral sphere refer to his *doing*.

The question then is: How, in experiential terms, does the state of separation come about and what does it mean? Quite apart from strictly theological issues surrounding the particular doctrine of original sin, the Christian answer to these questions is straightforward. Paul expresses the point directly in the opening chapter of Romans when he says, "Knowing God, they glorified him not as God . . . and changed the glory of the incorruptible God for the likeness of an image of corruptible man . . ." (1:21, 23). The state of separation or the basic deficiency of man consists, therefore, in a self-assertion that makes man and not God the basic orientation of the self—the object of supreme devotion. That this self-assertion reaches to the being of man and is not to be understood merely in terms of specific moral failures can be made clear by citing the ideas of two modern and very influential philosophers, Nietzsche and Sartre. That they both reject the Christian diagnosis of man's predicament and the setting of a limit to human self-assertion is not as important as what can be learned about Christianity from these very rejections. Nietzsche, who understood man's being in terms of a highly disciplined form of self-assertion or will to power, was forced to include "God" among the list of "lies" that accompany morality[1] largely because of his belief that man would be destroyed were he forced to acknowledge a divine power not only beyond himself but beyond all that he might become as the result of transcending himself through the *Übermensch* as well. In Nietzsche's writings we find one of the first expressions of an idea which has steadily increased in importance since his time; it is the idea that the being of God is a threat to, a negation of, man's being. Nevertheless,

---

1. See *Ecce Homo*, in *Basic Writings of Nietzsche*, trans. and ed., Walter Kaufmann, (New York, 1968), pp. 692-93. The same idea is expressed in many other of his works.

despite his bitter and relentless attack upon Christianity, Nietzsche was far from oblivious to the import of the Christian ideas. He understood that belief in man's guilt before God and in his consequent separation from God stemming from unbounded self-will reaches to the root of man's being and constitutes more than a moral failure.[2]

The point becomes even more clear in the case of Sartre and some other of the existentialists, where man's genuine existence in freedom means that he is to have his being solely from himself and not from another. Being self-created is one way of understanding the existentialist claim that existence precedes essence; if man were a being created by God he would then have an essence given to him by a power other than his own, something incompatible with authentic existence which includes both the freedom and the responsibility to project himself from himself. Sartre's rejection of God is therefore much more profound and illuminating than typical skeptical and anticlerical versions of atheism. It is, instead, the expression of a fundamental antithesis according to which the being of God and that of man mutually exclude each other. The underlying belief is that if God were a reality, man could not be, because man can be only insofar as he projects himself entirely through his own freedom, something which he could not do if he had been given an essence by a creator. Conversely, if man really is, in freedom and responsibility, then God cannot be; God's being would in fact be a *disaster* since it would reduce man to nothing. The full depth of the antithesis becomes manifest in Sartre's idea that the goal of man consists in the project to be God. "The best way to conceive of the fundamental project of human reality," he writes, "is to say that man is the being whose project is to become God."[3] And it is most instructive to notice that the conception of God Sartre has in mind is that of a powerful and autonomous being, wholly self-contained and in no need of another. There is no mention

2. See G. Van der Leeuw, *Religion in Essence and Manifestation,* J. E. Turner, trans. (New York, 1938), ch. 67.
3. Jean-Paul Sartre, *Being and Nothingness,* Eng. trans. of *l'Etre et le Néant* by Hazel Barnes (New York, 1956), p. 566.

of a God who cares or is concerned or who appears in the form of sacrificial love; there is only the God of power and of complete self-sufficiency. "The fundamental value which presides over this project [i.e., to become God]," writes Sartre, "is exactly the in-itself-for-itself; that is, the ideal of a consciousness which would be the foundation of its own being-in-itself by the pure consciousness which it would take of itself. It is this ideal which can be called God."[4] In short, the authentic existence for man is to have his being entirely from himself. The depth of this position becomes clear when we understand that it is far more than a theoretical denial of God in a sense that would leave everything else as it was before. Instead, God is now displaced and man takes over his function as creator.[5]

It may seem strange to follow the Pauline statement about sin as man's self-assertion against God with the views of two critics of Christianity. It is strange, but it is also instructive because thereby we see that these critics have understood, as Christians frequently have not, that the self-assertion of man in the face of God which Christianity takes to be essential, has to do with man's *being* and not simply with one moral failure among others. Protestantism has often failed in its understanding of faith at this point; some theologians have been unable to resist the temptation to identify separation from God with specific sins or moral failures illustrated especially by sensual and sexual pleasures. But the fact is, as Augustine pointed out so well in his analysis of *Concupiscentia*, inordinate desire is not understandable in terms of the body alone or our sensory nature. All human desire, regardless of its object, involves reason, self-consciousness and evaluation of the object or aim in question. The same holds true for that form of self-assertiveness issuing in rejection of a supreme object of devotion transcending man. We cannot miss the deep irony which emerges when we consider that, in Christian perspective, the existential flaw creating man's predicament—his self-asser-

---

4. Ibid., p. 566.
5. It appears that not enough attention has been paid to the question whether man's creating out of nothing is more intelligible to us than the same activity as attributed to God.

tiveness and drive to set himself up in the place of God—defines, in the perspective of a Nietzsche or a Sartre, the very ideal of human existence. But we cannot pursue the comparison further; more important is recognition that the Christian diagnosis of man's predicament concerns his being and status as a total personality as opposed to locating the flaw in some part or aspect of man's nature such as his special "faculties"—understanding, feeling, will, etc.

Having isolated the flaw or factor that separates man from God and from what he was meant to be, it is necessary to consider more closely the nature of that flaw, whether it is internal to man or external in the sense of belonging primarily to the structure of the world regardless of what man may be or do. To be clear on this point is essential because there are two features about the conception of man's flaw or need which determine the entire structure of any religion. First, the precise nature of the flaw must concern both its status—whether it is internal or external to the human self—and what I shall call its "tractability" or recalcitrance. Does the flaw inhere in the nature of existence itself quite apart from anything man may do or say? Is it a necessary feature of man's existence? Is it an accidental or contingent affair so that it may exist for some creatures but not for others? To what extent is the flaw plastic or open to manipulation? How is it to be removed, neutralized or overcome? To what extent can the being infected by the flaw remove it through his own resources? To this question especially we must return because it focuses sharply on what I have called the "circular predicament" or the situation in which the being in need becomes aware that he is in need, but at the same time is led to consider whether he still has resources within himself for overcoming that need. Second, since the recognition of the flaw leads necessarily to the quest for a means of deliverance, our understanding of the nature and office of the deliverer is intimately related to our conception of what the deliverer must overcome and how it is to be accomplished.

The Christian conception of sin represents its diagnosis of man's flaw and the circumscription of his predicament. Let us seek to gain an experiential understanding of this diagnosis by analyzing it both in itself and in comparison with two other diagnoses of man's situation, one religious and the other secular in character. In Christian perspective man's flaw and need are internal to himself in the sense that he is responsible for the orientation, the stance and the attitude exhibited in his having made himself and not God into the supremely worshipful Being. The separation from God is thus a self-separation. The realization of this situation implies that we are aware of a standard—in Pauline and traditional theology it is the divine law which supplies this norm—in comparison with which we fall short or "miss the mark." Our self-knowledge as manifested in *conscientia*, which is a participating or engaged mode of knowing, apprehends the gap between what we are and do and what is demanded of us by the divine law. The location of the flaw in man's self-assertion thus makes it internal, something which is not derived from the structure of the natural environment. We may illustrate the consequences of such self-assertion by attending to human communities and institutions and the historical role they play in developing man's self-assertive character; the state of separation as the character of man's actual experience, however, is not itself to be derived from these historical conditions. In finding the root of this separation in man's self-activity, Christian faith sets aside two other alternatives; first, it denies that the separation is a necessary feature of any ontological structure since it belongs to the dimension of freedom, and second, it denies that it is an accidental affair in the sense that the separation is said to belong to man as such and not merely to this or that individual. The position is self-consistent because man's self-assertiveness in freedom goes beyond the alternatives of *necessity* and *contingency*, just as freedom transcends and at the same time includes both poles. The peculiar character of human freedom serves to underline the point that for Christianity man's separation from God and from his essential nature is a self-separation, since, apart from God, only in human freedom do we find exhibited the transcendence of necessity and contingency. Only in man's freedom does such a form of responsibility occur, for where necessity rules and all is determined by what is extrinsic to man there is and can be no responsibility, and where contingency rules so that imputation has no meaning there is likewise no responsibility. Christianity sees man as acting both freely and responsibly and thus as standing beyond the polarity of necessity and contingency. But the crucial temptation is found precisely at this point, because to stand beyond that polarity is to be like God and even to take the place of God. But we must not pursue the ontological account further; the experiential concern requires only that we emphasize the internality of man's flaw in man himself. It is for this reason that, in understanding faith, we speak of man's circular predicament. When man is aware of his predicament he cannot simply view it as one more theoretical or objective truth about the world because he is the one who is *in* the predicament and must face the question whether he can escape from it under his own power.

Since, as I have suggested, we must learn to understand faith in relation to alternative views, the internality of man's need or flaw from the Christian perspecitve is made more perspicuous when it is set in relation to other diagnoses of man's situation. On the one hand, we find in the classical Buddhist position a subtle insight into the human condition which includes a quite specific view of man's flaw, but one in which it is not entirely internal to man's being. On the other hand, we find in the Marxist diagnosis of man a decided emphasis on the externality of the flaw, insofar as that position acknowledges any basic flaw in man at all. The primordial apprehension at the base of the Buddhist faith is the apprehension of suffering *(dukkha)*—including physical pain, mental anguish, sorrow and frustration—as the lot of all sentient being. In the belief that, as the Buddha declared, "Birth is indeed a great evil" there is no hint whatever that man is in any way responsible for the structure of sentient life from which evil stems. Suffering is just "there" as a brute datum; it is the characteristic feature of existence. The second insight of Buddhism appears as somewhat enigmatic and leads us to reconsider the first. The cause of suffering, according to the second truth, is our attachment to existence and our inordinate desire or craving for more and more sentient satisfaction; if this truth is taken strictly it implies that man is responsible for the suffering which exists and is to be traced back to the fact that he was born. Whether both truths can be maintained consistently, is not necessary for us to decide; the relevant point is that Buddhism diagnoses man's flaw as belonging to man himself insofar as his desire is inordinate and he wrongly directs that desire to what is transient, impermanent and gratifying to the senses. The contrast which can be drawn with Christian faith is instructive; whereas man's flaw or self-assertiveness in the biblical view is seen as an internal self-will that seeks to establish itself against God, the Buddha sees no such contrast. Man's flaw is in his failure to overcome craving and in his misguided attachment to those ephemeral gratifications which cannot really satisfy him as an integral being. But there is no sense of man's rebelling against a divine reality. The flaw in man according to the Buddhist diagnosis is internal insofar as both the boundlessness of desire and the fact of man's attachment to what is impermanent are attributed to a failure of human choice. Though internal, however, the need is "tractable" in the sense that it can be overcome in the Noble Eightfold Path of discipline and insight that enlightens the eye and shapes desire in the proper way. On this view, the being in need is, in principle, capable of overcoming his need though, to be sure, the way is not easy.

By contrast, the Marxist secular diagnosis of the human condition focuses attention exclusively upon historical factors encompassing all of man's relations with his environment, and it is difficult to see that there is room for the sense of a flaw internal to man's nature as such.[6] Two reasons may be cited in support of this conclusion; first, most interpreters of Marx have taken him to deny that man has an essential nature which is given or fixed. Instead, man is conceived as creative self-activity *(praxis)* accom-

6. For good accounts of the Marxian view of man, the reader should consult Vernon Venable, *Human Nature: The Marxian View* (New York, 1945) and Gajo Petrovic, *Marx in the Mid-Twentieth Century* (New York, 1967). Venable's treatment emphasizes the classical Marxist interpretation, while Petrovic writes within the context of Neo-Marxism, stressing the humanism of the early Marx reflected in the manuscripts of 1844.

panied by consciousness and aimed at producing the means of subsistence. Since, moreover, this activity is manifest in, and helps to determine, the course of history, man himself comes to be seen as a social history. If, however, man has no essential nature, but is, rather, self-wrought in history, it does not seem possible to speak of a flaw internal to man as such. In describing the Marxist view of the contradictions and injustices inherent in the modern industrialist system, Venable writes: "This is a situation which historical materialism ascribes *not to the malice of modern men*, but simply to the current system of property relations."[7] And, indeed, this is a consistent position if individuals are, as Marx once wrote in the preface to *Das Kapital*, "personifications of economic categories." For in that case we have an impersonal system of economic, social, and political relations and, while distortions may be acknowledged to exist in the system, they are not to be accounted for by any internal flaw in man himself. It is, moreover, difficult to find in the Marxian diagnosis a conception of a flaw internal to man, because the human alienation of which Marx speaks is often described as the phenomenon of a historical epoch in which the total politico-economic situation is made responsible for man being separated from the products of his own activity, from himself and from other men. Considerable confusion surrounds this point and among Marxists many interpretations of alienation are to be found. It is clear, however, that insofar as the distorted character of man's actual life in the world is attributed to historical conditions—economic, social, etc.—there will be no tendency to find a flaw internal to man himself.

Despite this fact there is a parallel in Marxist thought to the Christian conception of sin; Archbishop Temple was not without grounds for his provocative insistence that Marxism presupposes the Judeo-Christian tradition and must be accounted a Christian heresy in the sense that it is a thoroughly secularized interpretation of religious categories. The parallel appears in the doctrine of alienation. Difficult and multifaceted as this concept has proved to be, it does point to a diagnosis of man's situation which

7. Venable, op. cit., p. 109 (italics added).

is at once realistic and cognizant of the ambiguities which must exist for a self-conscious being. Central to the many connotations sustained by the term "alienation" is that of the estrangement of man from himself: man ceases to be what he could or might be and is separated from his true nature. Despite the claim of Marxists that man has no "essential nature," the fact remains that the doctrine of self-alienation cannot be made intelligible without some indication of what the alienated self is alienated from. In short, it must be supposed that there is an ideal form of human existence from which man is separated and which he is prevented from realizing because of prevailing historical conditions. This is in fact Marx's view; it has been recovered in recent years by those who have focused attention on the early Marx whose language and moral passion were more that of a Hebrew prophet than of a political economist of the nineteenth century. But though the distortion in man's historical life is recognized, the root of that distortion is not located in man himself but, rather, in external factors derivative from man's existence in the world. Marx detected the ideological flaw in this or that philosophy or in this or that group's vested interest; he saw the exploitative capacity of man against man and he grasped the self-deception that is possible in every human endeavor, but he refused to acknowledge a flaw in man himself. In this respect, for all his attack upon bourgeois ideals and values, Marx remained within the grip of the progressivistic optimism of the Western rationalist tradition. Man's predicament is definable only in terms of the historical conditions of his existence as an active, self-creative being; man himself is not the problem of man, and hence man himself can escape from his predicament through revolutionary activities over which he is the master.

The enormous degree of truth in the Marxist critique vis-à-vis the disasters of Western industrial society is not our main concern. The foregoing comparison of the Christian view of man's predicament with the diagnoses offered by Buddhism and Marxism was meant to underline one point—the *internality* of man's need or flaw as envisaged in Christian terms. The point is essential for any understanding of what Christianity has meant by the concept of sin or the separation of man from the ground of his being. The problem lies with man himself and his misuse of freedom; any strategy for overcoming that problem must be appraised in the light of the fact that the being in need is the same being whose historical existence is rooted in his self-assertiveness and continuing propensity to place himself at the center of things.

If the Christian diagnosis of the human situation is to furnish insight into the ills of actual life, that diagnosis itself will have to be made intelligible in experiential terms. Traditional theological accounts of sin and man's separation were too completely rooted in an antecedent *necessity*—whether in the form of God's decrees or the curse of Adam—which seemed to transform man into an automaton or reduce him to the status of a star or a stone. If man is a being of freedom and reason—and it would seem that only God would dare to create such a being—any account of his being which ignores that fact is bound to be unconvincing. If, in order to tell what purports to be the truth about man we are forced to describe him as if he were *not* the being of freedom and reason we know, but only one more object in the scheme of things, then our supposed truth becomes falsehood. The Christian claim is that man in his actual historical existence—the "natural man" of Pauline theology—is separated from what he was meant to be and that this separation itself is not the result of an ultimate necessity standing entirely outside of human freedom, but is intimately connected with the manner in which man actualizes that freedom in existence. To make such a claim intelligible so that it presents itself not as the bare repetition of an ancient dogma but as a contemporary challenge both to ourselves and to other diagnoses of the human predicament, it is essential that we find what William James called experiential cash value for the central concepts. Let us concentrate on two main points: the logical and existential conditions required for apprehending the gap or separation between man as he is and as he should be, and the sense in which this gap itself points to a flaw or need in man, justifying the diagnosis in terms of what I have called the circular predicament.

To begin with, *every* judgment to the effect that actual man is distorted in his existence, alienated or estranged, requires a *contrast* between actual man and some conception of what his ideal form should be. Job was unable to make out his case or even to grasp the nature of his predicament without having before him a conception of God which would make clear what existence for the righteous was "meant to be." No diagnosis of the human situation can be made without a similar standard or norm. Here all positions face exactly the same demand; either no evaluative judgment whatever is made on man's actual existence or it is necessary to claim some insight into what essential, ideal or undistorted human nature would be like. In Christian perspective this norm is provided by understanding what man was "meant to be" in the divine intention made manifest first in the law and then in the concrete embodiment of the law of love in Christ. Our perception of the gap between this intention for man and his actual existence is at the same time a perception of the flaw which stands in the way of the fulfillment of that intention. The perception takes the form of a comparison for which there are familiar analogues in ordinary experience. When, for example, we intend to make a particular object, we have before us not only an idea of the nature of that object but also the aim to make it exactly as we intend it to be. In short, our intention embraces both accuracy and excellence; it constitutes our standard. The actual object when fashioned is to be judged in accordance with that standard, and insofar as it fails to conform to the pattern, we are justified in saying that our object is not what it "was meant to be." The object in its actual existence is thus separated from the ideal for it which we had in mind. This analogy helps us to understand the concept of sin as the judgment that man is separated from his essential self or is estranged from what he was meant to be in accordance with the divine intention.

The question which naturally arises at this point is: What is the status of this intention which defines man's essential nature and how is it related both to man as he actually is and to the flaw in his being said to be responsible for his state of distortion? Does this essential nature reside entirely in God's intention and thus stand merely over against actual man with an infinite gulf between the two, or is there not, rather, some continuity between the essential and actual, such that we can see in experience some clues indicating that what man was meant to be is a *real possibility* even if the flaw prevents him from actualizing it through his own resources? Actual man, though characterized by the self-assertiveness that sets him over against God, is nevertheless still man, a being of understanding and of freedom; if we are to understand how he is to be transformed into what he was meant to be, the divine intention cannot be merely and wholly "other" to his actual being if such transformation is to be a real possibility. The meaning of a transformation as experienced is found in a move from some present actual state to a future state not as yet realized. Transformation means that something is to come about which is not yet. If the process is to be intelligible the future state cannot simply replace the present one; there must be some basis, some form of real possibility in the actual state which serves to explain the transformation. In short, if man's actual state is to be transformed, it must be *transformable,* and if we are to have any insight into the transformation, it must exist as a real possibility in actual man. If man's distortion comes about as the result of a misuse or misorientation of freedom, then the overcoming of that distortion must take the form of a reorientation of freedom, and we must presuppose that man in need is able to *respond*—in faith, in hope and in love, to whatever initiative may be taken from beyond himself for accomplishing the transformation. And *response,* in contrast with *reaction* which characterizes objects in the world, means freedom. This freedom, though distorted, is still freedom and forms the ground of the real possibility of man's transformation. Without it, the process of redemption would turn into a puppet show.

The focus on freedom, of course, raises at once a host of problems well known to both philosophers and theologians. Within the confines of an experiential approach, freedom must be taken phenomenologically, or as we actually encounter it in ourselves on occasions when we reflect on ourselves and distinguish what we are from what we might be—when we plan, intend, project an end in view, consider alternatives and choose one among many. The metaphysical question as to whether we are "really" free, and even what this means, is beyond our scope. But that limitation will not prevent us from making one crucial point about freedom that aids us in understanding the Christian diagnosis of man, especially in relation to the powerful philosophies of freedom on the current scene. That point is that since man is a finite being, his freedom is likewise finite and conditioned, but the fact of such limitation does not mean that freedom is either done away with or made illusory. This view stands in contrast to that held by some of the philosophers of existence for whom authentic freedom is quite unlimited. Man does not "have" freedom, so the formula runs, man "is" freedom. Nothing concerning man is "given." He has no essential nature unless it be that of making himself, his past is vacuous, the personal and social conditions necessary for his arriving at the point where he is responsible and can exercise his freedom have no effect whatever on that freedom. One of the truly remarkable consequences of the position is that whatever man chooses or projects in freedom is "good" because, by definition, that is what the authentic individual aims at. The emptiness of a freedom that tries to become unlimited shows itself clearly at this point. *That* a plan or project is an expression of freedom becomes the paramount concern; *what* the plan or project is either becomes insignificant or is assumed to be justified solely in virtue of the fact that it issues from such sovereign freedom.

At this point the uncompromising realism of the Christian diagnosis of man becomes manifest and is seen to be of vital importance. If Christian faith understands itself when it speaks of the separation from God that is sin or estrangement, it means to point to a range of human experiences which everyone may verify in and through his encounter with himself and with other selves. These experiences all involve self-conscious action in which freedom is at once presupposed and misdirected. Consider the following occasions: I claim to acknowledge a law which is to be binding on all men and at the same time secretly prepare to make an exception in my own case; I deceive myself in the supposition that I am in fact as good as the good ideals I say that I acknowledge, thus supposing that *saying* is the same as *being;*[8] I desire more to be understood by than to understand another, and either fail to enter into community or seriously impair a community which already exists; I fear for my own being and come to believe that I can preserve it only if others are reduced to nothing or made subject to my own will; I fall into despair through loss of faith in any source of power transcending myself. All these occasions are made possible by freedom and self-consciousness, but each illustrates misdirection of freedom because I have set myself in the center of the situation as an object of unlimited value and concern.

These situations represent the experiential cash value for the concept of sin or separation of man from God. They are an index of man's flaw in Christian perspective. It is to such situations that one must point when he seeks to understand or exhibit the Christian diagnosis of man in actual existence. It is not, however, with the bare occurrence or facticity of these human failures that we are concerned; more important is that they be seen as rooted in the basic misorientation of the one who exhibits them. This is what is meant by saying that the flaw is internal to man himself and that he is thereby caught in a circular predicament. Man is not here making a judgment about something other than himself; whenever anyone acknowledges that his distorted behavior stems from the misdirection of his freedom, he at once becomes aware of his responsibility both for that distorted behavior and for the misoriented basis from which it flows. We find ourselves caught in a circle of responsibility and the decisive question is: Can we who have the *flaw* escape from it under our own resources? Earlier, reference was made to the "tractability" of the need exposed in the diagnosis of man. Such diagnoses in the case of both other religions and secular positions have often led to the exposure of

8. It was the manifest gap between *saying* or *claiming* and *being* that led Jonathan Edwards to place the greatest emphasis on *practise* in his signs of true affections: "Reason shows that man's deeds are better and more faithful interpreters of their hearts than their words." (*Religious Affections*, J. E. Smith, ed., Vol. 2, Yale ed., *Works of Jonathan Edwards* [New Haven, 1959], pp. 409–10.)

a flaw that is tractable in the sense that it represents a deficiency which can be overcome by the same being who exhibits it. The Christian diagnosis does not find the flaw in man tractable in that sense, hence the acknowledgment of separation from God must inevitably lead to the quest for some form of deliverance.

Can we express in experiential terms why it is that Christianity regards man's flaw as a disability which is not tractable? A complete answer would require a detailed analysis of the structure of human life in the world and especially of the psychology of human personality. A crucial feature of the answer, however, is not difficult to state. A transformation in being is required; in traditional language, there is to be a casting off of the old man and a putting on of the new. What does this mean? At the outset we must distinguish between singular decisions and actions taking place on specific occasions and a course of life or basic orientation of the self as a whole.[9] The two are not unrelated because the content and quality of every singular action will reflect the course of life of which it is a part, and conversely, commitment to a certain course of life must manifest itself in the performance of certain deeds and the avoidance of others. Choosing and determining a singular action, however, differs from choosing a course of life or basic orientation, because in the latter case we are concerned with the direction of the self as a whole and thus with purposes, aims and attitudes which govern and direct the many events constituting a total life span. We are concerned here with what Tillich called the ultimate concern transcending in its ultimacy and comprehensiveness all finite and proximate concerns. From this perspective, the question is: How shall a being with an inveterate tendency to make himself into the object of ultimate concern change this orientation by an act of will? The depth of the problem becomes clear when we consider the self-referential character of the occasions upon which man's flaw becomes manifest. I am, let us suppose, prepared to acknowledge

9. See Edmund Husserl, *Formal and Transcendental Logic*, Dorian Cairns, trans. (The Hague, 1969), pp. 110–11, for the concept of an *intentional synthesis* that binds together an entire life.

the commandment of love as universally binding and yet I fail, in a given case, to act in accordance with that commandment, excusing myself on the ground that the circumstances I faced were extenuating. Or again, suppose that I find myself driven by a vague but nevertheless powerful sense of despair which leads me to suspend a course of decent conduct and to damage the reputation of a rival by a calculated lie. From the Christian standpoint, I must see both experiences not only as singular transgressions, but as deeds stemming from the fact that I have set myself up as an exclusive end above all ends. I am to change this orientation, but how is this change to come about, since I am the one who needs the change and also the one who is to effect it? The Christian answer is that in some deep sense I cannot will this change as one act among others, but must look beyond myself to another source of transforming power. For there is much evidence to show that every attempt to increase my resolve to change while I still continue to view myself as my own end has the result of increasing my self-assertiveness.

It does not seem to me to be helpful to anyone who understands this diagnosis to be told at this point that the resolution of his predicament is found in another realm involving transactions between God, Christ and the power of Satan and that as a result he can be transformed. For if finite freedom belongs to the nature of man, and man separates himself through the misuse of that freedom, it must be through its reorientation that he is transformed. In short, the process of redemption becomes unintelligible to us as beings of freedom if it is seen in terms of a process taking place out of all relation to our own will and freedom. Though we are exhorted by St. Paul to "work out our own salvation," we know that from the standpoint of faith we are unable to do so on the basis of our own resources. And yet, though misoriented, we are still creatures of freedom, which means that whatever transformation is possible for us must come *through* that freedom. Some response to, some appropriation of, some faith in the transforming power must be possible for us, and just as no one will seek deliverance unless he has first acknowledged his predicament in his own consciousness, the deliverance itself can have no meaning unless it confronts a person in his freedom and calls for a response on his part. For if that transformation were some sort of mechanical replacement of the heart of stone by the heart of flesh, what meaning would that have for our own consciousness? In being thus transformed we would be reduced to an object, to something other than our created nature, which is that of a person. Moreover, the continuity and integrity of a person as this being, once separated from and later united with the community of love, would be lost. Paul's description of his experience nicely illustrates the problem. "I live," he says, "yet not I, but Christ liveth in me." Both sides of the transformation must be stressed; the old self is transformed in faith and thus a new foundation is laid, but it is the same self that is thus transformed, since the present self, as illustrated by the experience of Paul and Luther, is aware of and experiences the contrast between the two.

A more cogent understanding of the Christian diagnosis of man's situation would be gained if we laid more emphasis on its experiential dimension. We must return to self-understanding and thus come to realize why the flaw of man is envisaged as residing in man himself. Any understanding of that flaw which roots it in external circumstances beyond the scope of freedom is, from the Christian standpoint, inadequate. Man cannot sustain himself, either individually or socially, on the self-assertive basis, because on that basis his freedom has a goal which harbors a flaw within itself. One might have thought that reflection on any sizable portion of human history with its evils, inhumanities and terrors, would suffice to make it clear that man himself is not worthy to be the object of an ultimate concern. If we supposed ourselves completely deprived of any knowledge of God whatever beyond the belief that God would have to be conceived as the supremely Worshipful Being, we could still be sure of one thing: man is not God. And the chief reason is that man is the one in need, the one in the circular predicament. And the one who needs to be delivered cannot be the deliverer.

Having stressed the internality of man's need, it is of vital importance not to misconstrue this feature, as Protestantism has sometimes done. When we think of the need of man as internal we are likely to suppose that this means a pointing to each individual in nominalist fashion, one at a time. Or we are likely to suppose that seeing the need as internal sets it over against the *social* dimension of all human life as something external. The result is a monstrous confusion. Christianity expresses the utmost concern for the individual, to be sure, but it is not on that account to be interpreted as individualistic. In the New Testament, Jesus interprets the care which God has for the creatures not in terms of their sheer individuality, but in terms of their actual or potential membership in the *kingdom* of God. No individual stands all by himself as if he neither knew nor had need of another; the structure of created life excludes any such possibility. Early Christianity took cognizance of this fact, even if it has been forgotten over the centuries. The togetherness of individuals, the social dimension of life, is essential. And the consequence of this fact for historical life and experience is that, in diagnosing man's need, we are forced to recognize the extent to which corporate life—social, political, economic—is itself infected by the misorientation of freedom. The flaw in man extends to the limits of his historical life, a point often missed by Christian individualists who understood sin solely in terms of the failures of other individuals. Hence the error of the frequently repreated antithesis between "saving" individuals and redeeming society. This is a false antithesis, false both to Christianity and to the facts of historical existence. Man exists in groups, communities and organizations as well as in his individuality. If, in Christian perspective, man as an individual exists in separation from God, his corporate existence is also alienated. For all of its theological shortcomings, the "social gospel" of four decades ago grasped this truth; it was a prophetic movement on Christian ground because its adherents perceived the evils inherent in our social life and refused to believe that they manifested nothing more than a great many individual failures multiplied. Just as man exists in community, distorted man exists in community; Christianity knows this to be true even if Christians have often overlooked the fact. Hence we must not identify the internal character of man's flaw with a distortion in man as an individual, at the same time supposing that conceptions of the flaw as external must always focus on some form of social distortion. Individual and social go together; wherever man exists there also exist individuals and communities. Therefore, every understanding of faith in which it is supposed that an individual is "saved from" society, the world or civilization is mistaken. Man is to be redeemed from himself in every dimension and at every level of his existence, and this means that the disoriented community is as much a matter of concern as the most isolated individual.

In the end, the most important feature of the Christian diagnosis of man is its existential or prophetic character. For here understanding means judgment; whoever understands the diagnosis also understands that it concerns himself and his own being. But the understanding must be experiential in character and not merely "notional," as Edwards and others have pointed out. Each individual has at this point to comprehend faith in and through self-examination, otherwise one is left with nothing more than the knowledge that Christianity makes a certain claim about the human situation. Authentic experiential understanding, however, drives us to the application of the diagnosis to ourselves and leads on to the quest for the power that can resolve the human predicament. Only if there is acknowledgment of the need and an understanding of its nature does that quest become intelligible.

V

God as Transcending Center
of Intention

A candid appraisal of our present religious situation reveals one basic fact: many people, including countless members of Christian churches, have lost the *sense* of God's reality because they cannot honestly say that they understand in their own experience what or who they are talking about when they use or hear the term "God." Some theologians have expressed alarm at this state of affairs, but its positive aspect must not be overlooked. The honesty manifested is a sign of genuine concern, and who can deny that, in the midst of so much sham and self-deception in modern life, it is salutary to encounter those who want to avoid dishonesty in religion. The present bewilderment about God, the popular talk about the "death of God," and references by social scientists especially to the "post-Christian era" must be understood as the inevitable development of a highly skeptical and secular consciousness extremely powerful at present in the Western nations.

Three factors are of special importance for explaining this outcome. First, the undisputed success of science and the very considerable extent to which that curious combination of science, myth and metaphysics sometimes called the "scientific outlook" has established itself in our processes of thought have led many to believe only in those realities which disclose themselves to observationally controlled sense experience, or are needed for the explanation of physical, chemical and biological processes. In this perspective, God appears, as he did to Laplace, as no more than a hypothesis for which we have no need. God becomes the victim of the principle of parsimony, better known as "Ockham's razor." Moreover, narrowly empiricistic thinking represented in earlier decades by logical positivism and more recently by some forms of linguistic analysis sets up criteria for the meaningfulness of every expression in terms of verification in sense experience. On these views, not only is the term "God" literally without sense, but it is doubtful whether the term "person" is meaningful either, except as something which is identical with the body. Second, the extended discussion about the existence of God in modern thought, and the focusing of the issues around the concepts of existence and nonexistence have had the effect of obscuring the question of the *nature* of God. The question whether there is God has often overshadowed any clear understanding of what reality the argument is about. My impression is that much of the current skepticism is to be traced to this source, for even if we reject, as we must, the demand that the term "God" be subjected to the empiricist's meaning criterion narrowly construed, the fact remains that we must mean *something* intelligible by the term. If God is not to be understood as one more object in addition to all the objects there are, then we shall have to find some other concept, Being, Person, Spirit, which will serve to fix our attention and express our intention when we speak seriously about God. Third, our problem is aggravated rather than resolved by the supposition that we need only abandon philosophical analysis and speculation and return to the revelational language of the tradition, as if it were perfectly clear what is meant when we utter such expresssions as "I believe in God the Father Almighty" or "God appeared unto Abraham, saying. . . ." The positivists were wrong in their ultimately dogmatic stance about the meaninglessness of theological concepts, but they were right in their demand that we wrestle with the problem of what we do mean when we engage in what is now called "God talk."

The point I want to emphasize is the need for interpretation and reinterpretation of the traditional theological concepts. The continuing effort must be made to recast these concepts in terms of experiential analogues which show their relation to our life in the world. Some degree of sophistication is called for, since we are dealing ultimately with the two mysteries symbolized in faith by the Alpha and the Omega, the ultimate *from whence* and *to whence* of all existence. There is to be seen a curious twist in the modern mind at this point; whereas few would suppose that the most abstract and theoretical concepts in science—antimatter, negative spin, reversible time—can be understood in terms of our gross and naïve experience with ordinary objects, it seems to be taken for granted that the theological concepts can and should be interpreted in just such naïve terms. Perhaps the supposition is that in this way their meaninglessness can best be disclosed. Behind this attitude stands the deep split in modern consciousness between what are sometimes called matters of knowledge and matters of value. Knowledge which can be supported in experimental fashion is confined to the special sciences and sealed off from the comprehensive frames of meaning—moral, religious, esthetic—which interpret life and give it purpose. These meaning frames, it is said, are not matters of knowledge and represent no more than personal preferences, conventional opinions or emotional expressions. Some theologians have accepted this bifurcation as philosophical truth in the hope that by a sort of gentleman's agreement they may be allowed to preserve their revelational theology intact and secure. What matter, they say, if our theology is excluded from the sphere of what secular man calls knowledge, for have we not in our possession the knowledge which is God's? Moreover, they claim, what damage is done if we say that of course faith is a matter of personal preference, it is the personal preference of all Christians who understand God, man and the world in terms of what the Christian community believes. In reply, we must say that the matter and the damage are evident on every side; theology becomes encapsulated in a water-right container of its own making and as a result appears more and more as a strange and foreign body to the men who dwell in the secular city. But there are in addition theological and philosophical reasons why the bifurcation in question cannot be accepted.

First, though we may and indeed must identify the faith we are seeking to understand with the deposit of knowledge which is God's, we still do not escape the stricture that, in biblical language, we have this deposit or "treasure" in "earthen vessels."

Moreover, those who possess this deposit exist in history and theology itself has a history, which means that the earthen vessels turn out to be the secular knowledge of a given time—philosophy, archaeology, church history, philology and, at present, even grammar. Without dependence on these tools we are unable to preserve the deposit, let alone succeed in understanding it. Second, and closely related, we may justifiably identify faith with what the church says or with what the Christian community believes, but when we come to assert it or commend it to the modern man, we shall have to interpret it in intelligible terms that take us far beyond traditional theological language. Difficult questions are not answered merely by repeating the language of creeds.

It was necessary to begin the discussion of God with what is likely to appear as a digression because it is imperative that we understand some of the factors in modern life which stand in the way of any attempt to speak intelligibly about God. Understanding obstacles, however, is not enough; we need to deal with the substantive issues even if we cannot do so without knowledge of the critical problems we must confront.

The task lying before us is nothing less than that of finding in our experience a basic analogy that will enable us to gain some understanding of the reality standing behind and beyond the term "God." An excellent place to begin is with the term itself. The term "God" may be taken in a dual sense; on the one hand, it may be considered as a name, and, on the other, it can be interpreted as a concept. A name does not merely denote or refer; to know what or whom it denotes we must know *something* about the reality meant. "God" is the name for the Creator and Sustainer of all things in biblical faith and, as such, that name denotes a reality understood in a distinctive way. That reality is variously described as the Holy One, the Father, the One who is Spirit and Love. Common to these descriptions is the central insight that God is, in some sense, a *person* or self, an *individual*, not a universal, a *personal reality*, not a principle, a *life* and not a substance. It is God understood in this sense for which we must attempt to find an experiential analogy.

The term "God," however, may also be taken to mean a concept and this point could occasion some difficulty. There are those who hold that "God" as a name attaches uniquely to the biblical God and they reject the idea that there is a generic concept of God such as would be involved in saying, as, for example, Whitehead does, that there have been three basic conceptions of God in human history: the idea of God as a sacred order, the idea of God as the One or absolute unity expressed in monism, and the Judeo-Christian idea of God as spirit or self-conscious individuality. Those who hold that the term "God" is a name and nothing more would reject any suggestion that it could be used to denote any reality other than the one referred to in the Judeo-Christian tradition. In short, they would deny that the sacred order or the One previously mentioned are conceptions of God at all, for the term "God" is taken as an exclusive or proper name referring to the biblical God alone. The matter is neither merely terminological nor pedantic; it points to a profound and inescapable problem concerning revelation. Earlier, I referred to the Christian deposit or content of faith as a historically *received* and experientially mediated disclosure of God which stands as normative for the Christian tradition. The key term here is "received." Those to whom the disclosure was made had to be able to receive it. And among the conditions for this reception was the presence in their minds of some conception of what they were looking for, that is, some conception of God. And to be in search of God requires that some idea, however vague, distorted or inadequate, of what it means to be God must precede any historical disclosure. In every record of such disclosure there is presupposed a generic concept of God which has as its minimal content the idea of a reality on which all there is depends, an ultimate reality not itself subject to the vicissitudes of existence as are beings which come into being and pass away. Augustine saw this point very clearly in the example cited in *De beata vita* of the sailor who recognizes his port when he lands although he has not actually been there before. The same point is implied in his repeated use of the expression "you would not seek me if you had not already found me." A part of the meaning of even the most unique and historically mediated disclosure of God, such as

Christianity maintains, is this generic concept of God derived from man's pervasive experience and reflection on the world and himself. This concept furnishes the clue which guides man's search and fixes in his own consciousness the belief that he is searching for that reality on which everything depends and not for anything else. To be sure, when the search is terminated in actual disclosure, we have come upon the concrete nature of God and our generic concept is reshaped in accordance with that historical disclosure. Our ultimate understanding of God is not limited to the clue presupposed at the outset, because that clue is abstract, being based on the pervasive traits of things without regard to the experience of historical communities such as ancient Israel or the churches of primitive Christianity. But without that clue there could be neither a quest nor an intelligible reception of the divine which signifies its successful completion. Since the generic concept of God is rooted in experience and the quest for God is also experiential and not a merely speculative endeavor, the actual disclosure of God becomes essentially related to experience. This important fact would almost certainly be overlooked if we confined our understanding of faith to formulas and verbal expressions. Such expressions are, to be sure, essential, but behind them are experiences and encounters which transcend all verbal expression.

Our aim now is to see whether we are able to reach understanding about the Christian conception of God by means of some fundamental analogy of experience. First, it is necessary to be clear about the main features of that conception, for, as I have often repeated, we do not intend to derive faith or construct it from experience, but rather, to understand faith by means of experience and thereby give it a new concreteness. The fundamental idea in the biblical conception is that God is to be understood as, in some sense, a self, a living self-conscious spirit who acts in and through history, through the cosmic order and in the human person. As such, God is to be understood as an individual; *the* individual, in fact, who transcends all finite realities in the sense of not being identical with any one of them individually or with all of them collectively. Whatever difficulties may stand in the way of our understanding what this means, neither selfhood nor individuality can be abandoned. Throughout the experiences of the major figures of Old Testament religion from Moses to the end of the prophetic line runs the image of God as a self-conscious spirit, one who speaks and acts, one to whom prayer can be addressed as in conversation, one who knows and judges, one who confronts man in anger and overcomes his alienation in love. The picture set forth in the New Testament is not essentially different. Jesus consistently refers to God as Father and in the faith of the primitive Christian communities it is clear that God was understood as an ever-living Spirit who knows and judges the hearts of men. Moreover, the classical trinitarian conception of God pointed in the same direction and was in fact an attempt to express the centrality of the personal. The use of the term *persona* to express the disclosure of God as Father, Son and Spirit testifies to this fact.

We must not ignore the obvious difficulties which such a conception presents for our understanding. We must, above all, avoid the simple and naïve conception of God as *one more* reality among others or as any sort of object among other objects, although it seems clear that such errors still persist. Some may recall the quite serious comment made by Mr. Khrushchev some years ago when the first astronaut completed his flight into outer space. He made a point of telling us that this man had flown higher than any previous human being, but that he did not find God or any such reality. On a more relevant level, the mystical tradition within Christianity has always been uneasy about the use of the concept of self in understanding God because of the sense that it qualifies God and reduces him to a finite reality incompatible with the divine majesty and transcendence.[1] Hence

1. A major source of confusion here is failure to distinguish being *finite* from being *definite*. If the term "God" had no definite meaning, or if it could receive definite meaning only in virtue of God's being conceived as finite, then, of course, nothing whatever could ultimately be said about God. But the confusion need not take place; *finite* and *definite* are different in meaning. The former contrasts with *infinite*, while the latter contrasts with *indeterminate* or *vague*. Thus there is no need to suppose that having a definite idea of God is the same as having a finite God.

it was characteristic of the Rhineland mystics, for example, to draw a distinction between the Godhead and what they called the God of the ordinary religious consciousness. The Godhead transcends all finite distinctions, involving predicates and relations, and therefore cannot be regarded as a self; this reality is to be approached only through mystical preparation ending in the sacred silence transcending speech. God, on the other hand, the self-conscious spirit, is seen as an appearance of the Godhead; the implication is that personality or being a self is not an *ultimate* characterization of the divine reality even though the image may be allowed as a concession to the man of simple faith. This way of understanding faith cannot be accepted even if it contains an important truth which helps us to avoid an error. Any understanding of God which would reduce him to the status of reality interacting on a level with other realities within the system of things is inadequate; the major problem for theology in any form and at any time is that of speaking about God in the only human and finite terms we have available without being misled into thinking of him as a finite reality wholly circumscribed by our concepts and language. On the other hand, it does not follow from the warning issued by mystics and proponents of negative theology that the only way to overcome the inadequacy of finite thought and language is to transcend both and rest with the ineffable. Nor is it clear why the attribution of selfhood to God should come in for special criticism since, according to the mystic, all of our human characterizations of God are infected with finitude. The curious fact is that of all the basic concepts which have been employed for understanding the nature of God, selfhood is the only one with which we have genuine acquaintance in ourselves for providing insight into what an infinite and transcendent self might be like. With regard to such characteristics as power, goodness and knowledge, understanding them as infinite depends largely on the *quantitative* comparison; man has some power, whereas God is omnipotent, and the contrast is between *some* power and *all* power. With regard to selfhood, however, we can apprehend a *qualitative* contrast. God, as I shall try to show, can be understood through the analogy of our experience of finite selves or personalities, but whereas a finite self or center of intention is not self-contained and manifests a contrast between its essential nature and actual existence, God as infinite self is always adequately self-related and exists as he essentially is. This is what was meant in the traditional philosophical theology when it was said that in God essence and existence are identical. The point is that, instead of looking upon the understanding of God through the concept of selfhood as the placing of limitations on God, we have grounds for taking precisely the opposite view. The self is the only reality in our experience which we can conceive of as being purposely related to *everything* that is, and it is precisely this possibility of universal relatedness which qualifies the self as a proper model for the infinite God.

The question, then, is: What is a self, what or whom do we experience when we experience a self? If we can answer this we shall be in a position to frame our analogy of experience through which we are to understand the God of faith. The proper starting point for any discussion of the self is a confession of humility; whatever else we know or believe we know, the fact remains that we are creatures who use the term "I" more often than any other substantive term, and yet no one of us can say with confidence exactly what we mean. Who or what am I? When I say "I" do I mean my body, and if so, how is it that a body becomes self-conscious of itself and raises the question of whether it is a body? Hence, although I am obviously closely related to my body there is at least a problem as to whether I am identical with my body. Perhaps when I say "I" what I mean is my thoughts, my desires, my hopes as a unified system of meanings which constitute my life. But, then, this system is embodied and has a certain locus in the scheme of things. My existence as a self is bound up with my body as that through which I express myself, a truth well recognized in the biblical symbol of the resurrection of the body. I, it would appear, am not identical with either my body or my thoughts; I have a body, but I am not my body, not least because of the remarkable transformations which can take place in the material of my body without loss of my identity as a person. I have thoughts but I am not my thoughts, since I can consider any one of them and decide whether to accept it or reject it, whether to have it determine my action or set it aside. Moreover, I am aware of *selecting* among my thoughts, desires and hopes, and in this awareness I see myself standing beyond these thoughts, comparing them, judging them and relating them to my aim in life, and thus I am not identical with any one of them. I must therefore be something other than either body or thoughts. What may this something be and how am I to lay hold of it?

Whatever answer we can give is to be found in experience, for in experience the self discloses itself to itself. What actually takes place in an encounter between two selves? What or whom do I experience when I converse with or work together with another person? What is there in or about you that answers to my conception of you as that unique person to whom I speak, and what is there in or about me that answers to your conception of me as a unique person? A standard answer to these questions and one which has had powerful support in modern thought is that I hear you speak, interpret the gestures you make, observe the patterns of your behavior, and then conclude that you must be a being with a mind just as I am. This answer leaves much to be desired, for, apart from the fact that identifying you as a mind does not adequately express your being as a person, there is the difficulty that this account exactly reverses what actually happens when any two of us encounter each other. I hear you speak and seek to understand what you say, I see and interpret your gestures and I attempt to grasp the import of the patterns of your behavior only because I already assume that all these manifestations proceed from, and are the expressions of, a *center of intention* which I think of as being you. There is no need for me to *infer* that you are or have a mind because the evidence I would use as a basis for the inference is significant only in virtue of my having already presupposed that it is the expression of a mind. I regard your speech and behavior as something intelligible to be understood by me because in my encounter with you I envisage all your actions as expressions of that center of intention. When you speak and I seek to understand, I do so by attempting to discover what *you meant* (intended) to say as a person with a purpose or an intent in view. I do not merely hear sounds, but I grasp words as *your* words, as a medium through which you are attempting to express yourself to me. In short, I experience you as a purposive center transcending your words even while you express yourself *in* them and I experience you *through* them. Your words I hear, your actions I see, but you as the *center of intention* expressing yourself I do not see. The point is even more evident in the sphere of action. Your deed is a public affair, but its motive and intention, those features which constitute its relation to *you* as a person and make it *your* deed, do not appear on the surface of the act and can often be discovered only with the greatest difficulty.

Can we now say more precisely what is meant by a center of intention and how such a center is the core of the self? Here again, for answers we shall have to resort to the experience we have both of ourselves and of each other. To begin with, to intend is to have a *purpose* to express, whether verbally or in overt action, some meaning or idea to be understood or interpreted. Such a purpose or intention may be quite specific and limited as, for example, in the writing of a letter or in the doing of a chore, or it may be an overall purpose embracing an entire course of life, an expression not of what we mean to say or do on this or that occasion, but an expression of what we *mean to be* as this individual—our fundamental aim and style of life. This aim and style represents what would be, for us, self-fulfillment or self-realization. Every human life is guided by such an intention; at times it seems clear and we are, as we say, self-possessed, and at others it seems somewhat dim or obscured and we feel distracted, disoriented and unsure. Our unity and identity as persons is constituted by the overarching purpose which we acknowledge as determining our lives. Kierkegaard had precisely this in mind when he described purity of heart as the willing of one thing. Our ultimate aim spans or endures through time and change and stands, so to speak, behind all that we do and say. That overarching purpose which both expresses and is a center of intention, the direction and thrust of an individual life, is what answers to you as an integral person when we encounter each other. It is a unifying and living unity which makes intelligible all of your expressions and actions on the human scene. To be that self and no other means keeping that center of intention in view and continually identifying yourself with it. Moreover, its development or working out in time delineates a unique individual history or career unified by the center it expresses.

Intending, meaning, purposing mark the definitive traits of the person. The center of intention and the overarching purpose mark the unity of the self through time, and the self's concern, care and love for that ultimate purpose constitute the identity of that self. Self-development is not a mere organic unfolding of potentialities and possibilities such as we find in the passage of an acorn from its planting to its fulfillment in the oak tree. Care and love enter in where human personality is concerned; the self literally finds itself in its ultimate aim, and loves that aim in the proper sense of self-love indicated by the commandment that we are to love our neighbors as we do ourselves. It is not sufficient to lay stress on the self merely as knower who can intend a certain thought content and verify its truth, nor even on the self as agent in purposive activity. A self is also a *center of concern* both for its own being and for the being of others; without that concern which extends itself to the destiny of the self as a whole, experience would reduce either to the process of theoretical observation and explanation, or to a series of discrete actions in response to each situation and challenge. The affective dimension of selfhood enables us to avoid both distortions. The loss of that dimension is reflected in the widespread loss of personal community and communion in contemporary life. The person is often viewed only as an object of study, or merely as a being to be controlled or manipulated. In both cases the fact that the person we study or seek to control is a being who loves and aims at the realization of his being is ignored.

Persons discover each other as persons through experiential encounters mediated by signs or language. The self to be known must express itself in a form which establishes intelligible relations with other selves. We have no access to knowledge and understanding of another person except in this mediated fashion;

forms of expression when interpreted and understood by other selves constitute so many intelligible links between us. Though the self expresses itself in signs, symbols and actions, these forms of expression, however, are not themselves identical with the self expressed in them. This is a vitally important point and one invariably ignored by the proponents of hard behaviorism. It is one thing to maintain that it is impossible to *know* each other as persons without behavioral expression, but it is quite another to *identify* the self with that behavior. There is no reason to believe that the *manner* in which something is known furnishes a sufficient index as to its nature. I experience your disapproval through the tone of your voice, the look on your face, the words you use in addressing me, but the disapproval as an intended meaning issuing from your center of intention is not identical with the tone, the look or the words. You are, to be sure, expressed in or communicated through those media, but in your self or person you transcend them. And you transcend them not only in being aware of what you intend to express through them, but also in virtue of your being as an overarching purpose which is never exhausted in any single occasion or experience. Every occasion of expression which is purposive includes not only the specific content communicated, but also the fact that it was intended. Thus the center of intention as such transcends any one of its specific manifestations. With regard to the overarching purpose constituting the center of the self, moreover, no single occasion of expression exhausts it. This element of transcendence is essential if we are to succeed in our attempt to employ the analogy of our experience of selfhood for understanding the nature of God.

We have seen that, for Christian faith, whatever else is to be said about God, the character of personality, of being a self or a self-conscious spirit, is central. My proposal is to understand the biblical God as personality, an infinitely transcending center of intention, being expressed through the world, through man and through history in the special form of revelatory events culminating in the revelatory person which is Christ. In confronting those who fear that "God is dead," it is necessary to underline the fact that, in Christian perspective, God is a self, a living, spiritual center whose intention is expressed in all that is and whose unity and identity reside in the constancy of an overarching purpose. And in speaking thus about God, one is not speaking about a principle, nor is one speaking about one more object among the objects we know, nor again does one have in mind a pervasive unity in or of the world. Instead, the reference is to the infinite, living, spiritual self whose intention is expressed in the whole of reality including the cosmos, man, together with Christ and the Beloved Community which he established. And just as we do not identify finite selves with their expression of themselves, we also do not identify God with his expression of himself. This means that God transcends the world and indeed every finite reality without ceasing to express himself in and through everything that is. We shall consider in the next chapter the special significance of Christ as the manifestation of God's intention to overcome the world and man's circular predicament, and in the final chapter, the manner in which this intention is to be accomplished through the founding of the Beloved Community. For the present, I want to concentrate on the fundamental conception of God as the transcending center of intention.

Following our analogy of experience in the attempt to understand faith, we began with the thesis that selves are known in experience through conversation and through encounter. What there is, what Locke called the entire furniture of the universe, is seen from the perspective of faith as the expression of God's intention, which means that the cosmic order, including man and human history, constitutes a language, a set of signs and symbols, which are to be read and interpreted as revelatory of that divine self. Just as we came to comprehend each other through the signs we used to express ourselves, so we come to comprehend God through the medium of signs and symbols. Through our experience of the physical world we come to know the structure and function of the divine *Logos* which is at once both word and pattern or form. That is, we detect this *Logos* in the things, and we see it as the expression of a center of intention which transcends both those things and the *Logos* itself. There is a divine center who means or intends that *Logos;* it is not just "there," but is the expression of a reality beyond itself. A contrast between ancient Stoicism and Christianity is instructive at this point. The striking feature of the Stoic *Logos* is found in its status as an immanent rationality, whereas in virtue of the biblical doctrine of creation, the *Logos* appears as that through which all things were made by God and hence as manifested in the world, while having a source *beyond* the world. Through our experience of the events of history and the patterns of the historical order, there opens up another channel through which the transcending center is disclosed. The historical medium is the language of the divine self, to be deciphered in a twofold way. On the one hand, there is a canonical record in the biblical documents, a record which preserves in the words of several natural languages the religious insight which embraces the world, man and the course of history. In that record is expressed the series of encounters or dialogues between the divine self and the men of faith through whom the intention of that self was expressed. Those encounters extend from the theophanic experience of Moses through the long history of the prophetic tradition to the disclosure of the divine intention in Christ. The results are there as once deciphered in the biblical record, which is to say that that record itself represents a casting into language of the interpreted meaning of the experiences and events which form the substance of the biblical content. The other side of the twofold deciphering appears in the fact that the biblical record itself needs to be read and interpreted. The point is not to lay stress on the problems of interpretation, but rather, to underline the fact that historical experiences and events plus the word which interprets them are *languages* expressing the transcending center of intention. Through those languages and their interpretation the divine self comes to be disclosed.

In surveying the record of this self-disclosure, three points in experience are particularly well focused. First there is the *prophetic voice* in and through which the essential features of the divine intention are made manifest. The second is found in the phenomenon of *conscience,* where the divine intention in the form of the law exercises judgment *in* us, revealing the discrepency existing between what we do and are and what we were meant to be. The third takes the form of the singular expression of the divine intention for overcoming the world in the figure of *Christ.* Each of these phenomena can be interpreted in terms of the basic analogy of two selves expressing themselves through various media which serve as signs enabling each to penetrate the center of intention which defines the other. Behind these phenomena stands the transcending center of intention; the situations I have cited are important not merely in themselves, but primarily because they are supposed to *point to or mean God.* If this fact is omitted we are left with nothing more than a historical record of experiences which may be of some interest to historians but are without revelatory significance. To put the point most strongly, we are concerned with Christ not merely in his own being as a historical personage, but because he is meant to disclose the nature of God.

The prophetic voice furnishes the clearest illustration of dialogical disclosure of the divine center in experience because the prophet through his role is one who "speaks for" that center. The prophet, that is, reads the expressive signs of the times in the historical order and interprets them as expressions of the divine will. He speaks the interpreting word and at the same time feels that the word is spoken through him. Consider the example of Hosea who, like the other great prophetic figures, used analogies of experience to express religious insight. Hosea was well aware of the meaning to be attached to the concept of the divine justice symbolized by the figure of the plumb line made vivid by his predecessor, Amos. Hosea knew the implications of that concept applied to the conduct of his unfaithful wife, and yet he could not believe that a symmetrical form of justice which exacts equal payment for transgression adequately expresses the intention of the divine self. A struggle took place within him which he transposed into a struggle within the divine consciousness itself; the result was disclosure of a redemptive loving kindness at the heart of the divine intention. "And Jahweh said unto me, go again, love a woman . . . even as Jahweh loves the children of

Israel though they turn unto other gods" (Hosea 3:1). The dramatic reversal which takes us beyond justice as something self-sufficient is expressed in the moving verses of the 11th chapter, where Jahweh asks, "How shall I give thee up, Ephraim? How shall I cast thee off, Israel?" (11:8), and goes on to declare that his heart is turned; the execution of the divine wrath is stayed, and the reason given is one of the most candid utterances in all religious literature: *"for I am God and not man"* (11:9). The clear implication is that the divine intention is not identical with nor exhausted by the justice which merely repays; there is another dimension in that intention and it aims at the recovery or transformation of the one who fails. We have here a pure case of the prophetic reading of signs expressed in the form of experience; Hosea's experience serves in this case as a divine language, just as did the visions of Amos and the insight of Jeremiah under his almond tree. Our proposition is that these experiences and their interpretation are expressions of the transcending center of intention; they make clear what we understand faith to mean when it speaks of the disclosure of God in the historical order.

The second phenomenon in which the dialogical expression of God or the transcending center manifests itself in human experience is in the phenomenon of conscience. This phenomenon finds classic expression in the experience of Paul and is verified in the experience of every human person. Much confusion has surrounded past discussions of conscience; the main difficulty is found in uncritical use of the metaphor of a "voice" regarded as an infallible oracle and speaking truth in a wholly intuitive way. Etymology, while neither as instructive nor as oracular as Heidegger seems to think, does furnish important clues. The Latin *conscientia*, like the Greek *syneidesis*, implies a capacity for *self*-judgment that is, a form of knowledge in which the self is able to apprehend and compare its own actions and the direction of life as a whole with a standard representing what it ought to do and to be. This knowledge is peculiar in that it has an *affective* side in the sense that the awareness of a discrepency between what is done and what should be done is *experienced* as painful, as a state from which we want to escape. Logically, the judgment of conscience has two sides; on the one hand, it requires a *universal* in which the standard—for example, the commandment "Thou shalt not kill"—is set forth as defining an action which is everywhere and always forbidden. This standard must be related to specific deeds, such as executing a criminal or killing an enemy in battle, which are regarded as falling unambiguously under the scope of the standard. Second, there is the *individual* or personal side realized when the individual makes a judgment upon himself which, in the nature of the case, must be made by him and no other. The ambiguities of judgment are at once apparent. Judgment is not a straightforward deductive process but a creative act; when we are given a universal rule meant to apply to specific cases we must not expect to be given another rule which dictates precisely whether a specific instance does or does not fall under the original rule. For example, we cannot avoid such questions as, Do *all* instances of killing human beings fall under the commandment? or Are some cases peculiar and conditioned by special circumstances? There can never be a rule which dictates the *application* of a rule in a way that determines an individual decision absolutely. This is the reason King Solomon was famous for his wisdom. Individual decision can never be avoided, a fact which explains why conscience must always be associated with an utterly personal character. We misunderstand conscience, however, if we think of its individual side only in terms of "freedom of conscience," as if the judgment it expresses were mere whim or uncontrolled preference. We should speak instead of "freedom *in* conscience," thereby calling attention not only to the element of indeterminacy which is involved in every judgment, but to the control exercised by the standard as well. The Reformed tradition in Christianity knows both these features of conscience and may even be said to have made them decisive for faith.

The ambiguity of conscience, however, would not arise in the first instance were men not capable of comparing themselves with the divine standard set before them. The encounter with conscience in the individual is a critical point at which a finite center of intention encounters the transcending center or God in the form of the law. This encounter appears quite clearly in the experience of Paul when he makes the well-known confession, "the good that I would, I do not, and that I would not, that I do" (Romans 7:19); "Oh, wretched man that I am . . ." (Romans 7: 24). It is important to notice that this insight extends beyond the consideration of any particular act and is meant to describe a structural pattern manifest in the human situation as such. The judgment is made on the self as a whole, exposing man's actual falling short of the standard established by the divine intention. A peculiarly complex relationship between the two selves, divine and human, arises at this point. Without some expression of the divine intention, Paul would not know what was required of him or what standard he was meant to abide by. On the other hand, Paul had not only to apprehend and acknowledge that intention as disclosed through the law; he had also to know his own actual state and acknowledge the fact of its failure to accord with God's intention. And, as was pointed out previously, the experience of this discrepency is an affective one; Paul does more than "take note of" the fact that he has fallen short, for, as Edwards would have said, his "heart is some way inclined," so that he describes his condition as "wretched" and seeks to be free of it. In discovering himself and his actual situation, Paul encountered in his own experience the divine self as expressed in the intended norm for man. More is involved than the failure of Paul's life to accord with a standard or principle; his finite self *exists in contradiction* to what the divine self intends for him. It is in this sense that his life, caught in the circular predicament, is set against the divine life, and Paul experiences this opposition. The sense of an opposition between two selves and two intentions could not exist if the law were regarded not as the expression of the divine self and intention, but only as a set of universal prescriptions.

The third and, in several senses, final expression of the transcending center of intention in human experience and history is the total phenomenon of Christ. This expression, as is indeed obvious, stands at the center of the faith to be understood. In Christ we have the most concrete manifestation of the divine self as such—that God is the self of love—and also the manifestation of God's intention to overcome the world. Christ is the ultimate *language* through which the divine self is apprehended by us, and this in two senses: there is the language which Jesus himself *uses* in expressing his message, and there is also the language which he *is* in a total life, which could have been apprehended and interpreted only after his death and reappearance in the spiritual body (σωμα πνευματικόν). Christ as the language expressing the divine center of intention is mediated to us through the biblical record, although Christ himself transcends that record, since the ultimate object of faith is not that record but the reality it discloses. The plurality of languages involved points to a world of selfhood, since only a self can intend and only a self can have language as a form of self-conscious expression. I shall consider more fully in the next chapter the being of Christ as the final manifestation of God's transcending center of intention, a manifestation through which we encounter the divine self in history.

The peculiar fact about Christ is that in him *expression* and the *reality expressed* become one. God expresses his intention in Christ as a language which he transcends, but the word disclosing that intention is expressed not only in what Jesus *says*, which is a normal form of expression, but in what Christ *is*, or his total being. It is one thing to express the nature of something in propositional form and another to exhibit the thing itself. Thus it is one thing to *say* that the nature of God is *love* in a propositional form, and another thing to encounter that love in the form of the sacrificial being whose being is exhausted in love. The mystery of Christ resides in understanding how he can be both a language expressing the transcending center of intention and the embodiment par excellence of what that language means.

VI

Christ as Concrete
Manifestation of the Center

Paradoxically enough, Western philosophers at all concerned with religious issues have always been on better terms with God than they have with Christ. And one philosopher of the last century, when he was not being Dionysus, even set himself up as the Antichrist. No doubt the chief reason for this estrangement is the well-known "scandal of particularity" and the doubt which attaches to the claim of finality made in behalf of any historical being. It is not, however, my task to argue this matter from outside the theological circle, although I believe that a new perspective on the problem would be gained if philosophers avoided exaggerating the universality of reason and at the same time recognized the final claims they often make for historically conditioned philosophical traditions. And theologians should resist the temptation to appropriate for themselves the powerful traditional authority attached to classical theological language, especially when it cannot be made intelligible without massive reinterpretation. Therefore, it seems to me necessary to continue the enterprise of understanding faith in experiential terms in order to show what it means to attach religious finality to a historical person.

In the first place, the founder of Christianity is known to us only through the biblical record preserved and interpreted by Christian communities that continue to worship God in Christ's name. We confront certain accounts of a historical figure whose life embraces a message preached, certain deeds performed, and finally a sacrificial death which called into being what I shall call, following Royce, the Beloved Community. It is clear, however, that the record of the Jesus of history would not have come into being and would not have been preserved unless there already existed some faith concerning the significance of his being as a whole and the peculiar truth his life was meant to disclose. That faith took the form of a conviction that "God was in Christ reconciling the world to himself." Interpreting this claim in the terms I have been using means that Jesus is the concrete or historical manifestation of the transcending center of intention and that being an expression of that center is the same as being the Christ. His uniqueness stems from the fact that God intends him and that he *is*, therefore, the divine language; seen from the side of his historical being he *means* God. Jesus discloses the nature of the divine self in final form for Christianity and at the same time expresses the divine intention to resolve the circular human predicament. In encountering Christ one encounters the divine self expressing himself through another. Christ stands as the language which creates a community of understanding and of love between human and divine. And as with all language its being consists in being read, interpreted and understood; hence, our task is that of deciphering the meaning of Christ. The completion of that task, of course, cannot be accomplished in brief compass, but some basic points can be set forth that indicate the manner in which it should be done.

The aim is to find an interpreting word which expresses who Christ is and what he means. This word proves to be twofold; it includes the words which Jesus uses in setting forth his message as, for example, in the Great Commandment said to sum up the teaching of the law and the prophets, and it includes the interpretation of his entire life and being made by the primitive Christian communities and focused in the theology of Paul. Both words— the word of his historical message and the word concerning his being—are essential. Christ's significance is not limited to the words through which he expressed the teachings of his ministry, because his total import as the divine intention becomes clear only through the completed cycle of events known to those who came after him and could apprehend the significance of that cycle as a whole. The central word of his message is that a certain form of love constitutes the divine center and is the law of life. This means in turn that self-forgetting or sacrificial love is the only path to self-fulfillment. The central word of his being is that the resolution of man's circular predicament is the essence of the divine intention. This resolution is to be accomplished first by establishing the redemptive Beloved Community through a supreme act of self-sacrifice which exposes the error of human self-assertiveness, and second, by providing a channel whereby in faith and through that reversal of mind which is repentance, man may come to experience an acceptance by God which is in no measure based on his own acceptability.

These are interpreting words in the quite literal sense that they are conceptual formulations couched in language purporting to express what Christ means both in his message and in his being. But by themselves they are not sufficient, because it is the singular claim of Christianity that Christ is the one who is himself the concrete manifestation of the divine love. The interpreting word is required if we are to understand, but in the person himself we go beyond words to an embodiment of the truth to which they point. "I am the way, the truth and the life" (John 14:6) is a statement not to be taken lightly, because it points to the Christian belief that in addition to the propositional truth about God, there is also a direct exhibition of that truth in a singular being. The importance of this fact for experience is far-reaching; propositions we apprehend and interpret, but a person is a reality to be encountered. It is a great disservice to faith not to lay great stress on this concrete personality as a model of what sacrificial love is and means. And this model is not to be taken only as a relic of the past; on the contrary, it is a present living image to be encountered at every moment. Those who first saw the significance of Christ as a model and established the tradition known as *imitatio Christi* may have been excessive in their asceticism, but they were surely correct in availing themselves of the guidance which only a concrete model can provide.

If we look at this Person as a model of the sacrificial love which is to determine the pattern of life, three experiences stand out as fundamental in his life. There is, first, faith manifesting itself in what I call its *conative* side, as trust in or fidelity to the power and love of the divine self. Second, there is the loving regard and concern for the other or the neighbor, conditioned by the belief that the other is also loved by God. Finally, there is the utter self-forgetfulness, or emptying of the self before the divine self, which means the renunciation of any claim for one's own virtue or power in the sight of God.

The faith which Jesus possessed took the form of an unconditional trust in God informed by a clear conviction concerning his own message and mission. In terms of our previous analysis of the self, his preaching of that message concerning the divine love and the Kingdom of God and his unswerving obedience to the divine will represent his *overarching purpose.* In the constancy of that purpose is found his unity and identity as a historical figure. And throughout his ministry, even to the climax of his work when, as the text says, he set his face "steadfastly toward Jerusalem," his unity with the divine self is preserved. Nor is it broken at the crucial point where Christ is given over to death. The word on the cross which most closely approaches the tone of despair, "My God, why hast thou forsaken me?" is still spoken to "my" God, which is to say that the unity of trust in the divine self is not broken.

In his historical existence Jesus stands as a paradigm case of selfhood or personality. He has a firm grasp upon his overarching purpose, so that it informs what he says and does at every point. His relation to his purpose, moreover, transcends knowledge in the sense that he is related to it in love and loyalty and finally makes the ultimate sacrifice for its realization. A study of his teachings expressed in the various forms of language he employed—commandment, exhortation, admonition, judgment, parable, sermon, conversation—to communicate his message, leads to knowledge of the major deeds and events of his life. But neither the message nor the events exhaust his being. Beyond the words and the deeds stands his overarching purpose—the expression of the divine intention—which unifies and constitutes his being as that person and no other. Jesus stands as a unique and induplicable being because of the divine intention he expressed; knowing that he was obedient to it, one knows him through the purpose which controlled his life. We have here a dramatic model exhibiting the manner in which the integrity of selfhood depends on fidelity to a purpose. Jesus found his own life in losing it in the service of preaching about the love which casts out fear and makes possible the reconciliation of man and God. He reveals love as the law of life and shows the folly of every attempt to "save" one's life by withholding it, by withdrawing or by refusing to commit it in trust and love to an overarching purpose. Jesus' main command is for man to abandon the orientation which places himself at the center of life; instead, he is to trust the love which is God and the purpose envisaged by that love. He is fully aware of the risk involved, the contingency and uncertainty of every historical venture, the powers of evil, the sins of men, in short, all those obstacles which stand in the way of realizing in fact the divine intention both for him and for all men. He overcomes the powers in the end because of his faith—exhibited in trust in the power of the divine self—and his willingness to trust the evidences of things not seen. But Jesus could accomplish the task only because he had the sense and the conviction that the transcending center of intention meant to accomplish his purpose through him.

A second point at which Jesus discloses with peculiar clarity the intention of God is in the concern which he expresses for the other, or neighbor. Jesus saw each being as an object of the divine love and care, and as a consequence he treats everyone he meets not as a stranger, but as a neighbor in the sense made clear in the story of the Good Samaritan. The neighbor, though perhaps unknown, is not a stranger because he exists within a providential order and is encompassed in love and knowledge by the divine intention. Implicit in this outlook is the idea which defines the unique character of love (ἀγάπη) in Christian faith: to exhibit that love it is necessary to view the neighbor—his plans, his hopes, his fears, his needs—not merely from one's own finite, limited and distorted perspective, but to strive to see him and love him as he is in himself, which means as he is seen and loved of God. Jesus strove constantly to manifest this form of love, and he succeeded even in the most trying case of all, namely, in his attitude toward Judas whose treachery broke the unity of the community of disciples. He exhibited the same self-transcending love when he prayed for his crucifiers. In both cases Jesus saw the others through the love of an ultimate perspective which he both shared and embodied.

Love, not as the private feeling of liking, but rather as the sense of regarding the other in and for himself, represents what is most distinctive in the Christian outlook. The task is to show its relevance to the problems raised by conflicts and misunderstandings which divide person from person, group from group, and generation from generation. These forms of alienation stem from the failure even to attempt to see and love the other as he is seen and loved in an ideal perspective instead of merely from our own limited, interested and distorted perspective. The failure of love and insight leads us to see the other only in terms of our own interests and welfare, and even when we attempt to shape our conduct in accordance with a conception of what is "good" for the other, we are often projecting ourselves upon him and supposing that *our* conception of that good is final. But what of the real good of the other, his being and his destiny as envisaged from the standpoint of the transcending center of intention who intends, knows and loves him? The experience of the divine self includes a conspectus of the life of my neighbor and its meaning which is denied to me, but this fact does not release me from the obligation to keep that conspectus in mind as a standard exercising judgment upon my view of my neighbor. The commandment of love given and embodied by Jesus entails taking this self-transcending perspective into account in all our relations with the other who is now not a stranger but a neighbor. The peculiarity of the love which is *agape* is not adequately expressed in terms of simple contrasts between a selfish and an altruistic concern or between a sensual eros and a "spiritual" form of love. The true *agape* is a matter of gaining a self-transcending perspective; it involves seeing and regarding the other as he is seen and regarded by the divine self. God's intended good for the other keeps one from identifying his conception of what is good for that person with what is objectively and in truth good for him. My inability to apprehend this intention fully does not prevent it from exercising judgment on my own judgment. Jesus was able, to an extent surpassing our powers, to redefine the meaning of a neighbor because he looked upon all men from his new perspective as potential members of the Kingdom of God. His contemporaries, on the other hand, did not possess this perspective, which explains why they were forced to view men only in terms of their ethnic group, their geographical origin or their social status. Such categories are not without importance, but they are partial and finite; they concern only externals and fail to grasp the being of the neighbor which the agapistic perspective makes paramount.

That the love of which Christian faith speaks when it defines the relation between man and man is necessarily the law of human existence is foreshadowed in contemporary experience. Consider, for example, the massive misunderstanding between young and old that results in the well-known "generation gap." What was meant to be a community of trust and love—the family —has been broken into opposing forces and the tension has been heightened by an increased self-assertiveness on each side. Gradually there arises in the representatives of both generations a powerful sense not only of self-righteousness, but of self-protectiveness. The result is a tragic conflict in which young and old alike become encapsulated in their own standpoints, each believing that their being depends on the negation of the other. It is the consciousness that has been described as a frenzy of self-conceit; *I can be only if you are not.* Lacking in this situation is the perspective which Jesus manifests, the standpoint from which we see the other as intended and loved by God. As each is driven into himself and feels himself compelled to assert himself and to maintain himself in his self-assertiveness over against the other, the possibility of attaining the perspective from which Jesus saw the other virtually disappears. The urgent question is: How is the tragic conflict to be overcome and what will serve to re-establish the community of trust and love on the far side of its brokenness? Christianity claims that *somehow* Jesus in his office as the Christ makes it possible for man to escape from the destructiveness of his own self-assertion, to repent, to be transformed and to come to see the other once again as a being intended by the divine self. The many attempts made to interpret the work of Christ are so many attempts to say what the "somehow" means. And this brings us to the third focal point at which Jesus appears as the concrete manifestation of the divine intention. He represents God's intention to resolve man's circular predicament illustrated in the tragic separation of life from life. As the divine intention to overcome alienation, Christ assumes the role defined in our earlier analysis as that of the Deliverer.

Here we are brought to the edge of the theological problem of atonement and reconciliation. The problem in its full theological dimensions is beyond our scope. On the other hand, I have been emphasizing the experiential understanding of faith rather than its more strictly theological or speculative interpretation. Hence the problem is to express in terms intelligible to the modern man living within the secular city and its influence, what faith means when it speaks of Jesus as the Christ who atones. I should say at the outset that the traditional penal or satisfaction theories of atonement, quite apart from their reflection of biblical imagery and their formal consistency, are not well suited for contemporary interpretation. In the first place they seem to refer to a set of transactions taking place in another world utterly distinct from the one in which we live, and, second, these transactions, couched in the legal language of debt, the exaction of satisfaction, and the ultimate payment of debt, seem so completely out of touch with the actual consciousness of the man in the circular predicament that it is difficult for him to understand what they have to do with his present existence. What is it to our modern secular man that a God of vengeance long ago exacted a penalty from mankind which was ultimately paid by an innocent man? What has such an event to do with the problem of overcoming the self-assertiveness which separates man from the divine self? These are, to be sure, human questions, but a faith seeking understanding in terms of human experience cannot afford to ignore them. For what shall it profit us if we gain the whole world of traditional doctrine and lose the soul of understanding so that no one can appropriate the truth? This is not to say that traditional satisfaction theories represent so much error and that therefore we must swing over to the so-called imitation theories of atonement according to which the reconciliation of God and man is accomplished by a change in man's consciousness resulting from his encounter with Jesus. These subjective theories, so called, are, in my view no more acceptable theologically than penal theories are acceptable psychologically. The situation calls for reinterpretation in which, on the one hand, we attempt to maintain the continuity of faith and, on the other, to express it in intelligible terms.

Two conditions must be satisfied by any interpretation of Christian faith at this point. First, some event must happen, some deed must be done or some change must take place which is more than a change in thought or attitude. And the reason for this condition is clear: something which has been done—man's establishment of himself as his own ultimate end and the consequent alienation from God—has somehow to be nullified or overcome so that a reconciliation becomes possible. Since the flaw to be nullified exists as a real, historical power, and not only as a thought or an interpretation, the overcoming of that flaw must itself be a real, historical power. Second, since we are dealing here with human persons, beings of freedom and self-consciousness who transcend the world of objects and even themselves, the means whereby the flaw in man is overcome must be consistent with that freedom. If our aim were to synthesize some organic product or to produce a new type of missile, mechanical means would suffice both for the production itself and for overcoming any obstacles that might stand in the way. But the overcoming of the flaw in man presents a problem of a different sort. Where the goal is a reorientation of the self, self-consciousness and, as Kierkegaard called them, the existential movements of repentance and faith must be involved. No one is reoriented or transformed in the renewal of his mind merely by being *told* that some deed has made this possible. He must apprehend, appropriate, believe in or in some way relate himself to the atoning deed and to the one who performs it. Therefore, whatever form the delivering deed may assume it must allow for an appropriation on the part of the being who needs to be delivered.

Can we now say how it is that Christ is the concrete manifestation of the divine intention to resolve the circular predicament and how he fills the office of being the Deliverer? I believe it is possible to do so in experiential terms. I want to state what I take to be the solving idea first in its starkest form and then seek to develop some of its details. That idea is this: Jesus aims to overcome the separation between God and man and to re-establish the community of love broken by man's having set himself up as God; he accomplishes this through his own total obedience to the divine will, ending with the sacrifice of his own life so that the Beloved Community may be born and thus become the channel whereby man discovers the divine forgiveness and that he is once again accepted of God.

Jesus, to begin with, understands the human circular predicament. He knows that man does not orient himself toward the love of God and that he does not seek first the Kingdom of Heaven, but is bent instead on establishing the kingdom of himself. He knows, moreover, that just as the new wine cannot be put in the old wineskins, a new foundation for or reorientation of the self as a whole cannot simply be brought into existence by an act of will. And the reason for man's inability at this point stems from the fact that every attempt made to escape from the circular predicament by saving ourselves always involves a refusal to accept our guilt in separating ourselves from God, and a reinstitution of the same self-assertiveness which alienated man from the divine self in the first instance. On the one side there is the refusal to acknowledge the need to be redeemed, and on the other there is the belief that whatever redemption may be needed can be accomplished with our own resources. In both cases no reconciliation between divine and human takes place.

Is there, we may ask, anything that a man may do to effect a way out of the circular predicament? The answer of faith at this point is striking and it need not be expressed in too paradoxical a way. There is indeed something which a man may do, but it can be done only if he is not merely a man but the full embodiment of the divine intention. Christ, though a man, does what no ordinary man can do, he breaks through the circular predicament and re-establishes the community between man and God and between man and man through his unconditional fidelity to the divine will. This fidelity is most apparent in Christ's total emptying of himself—"not my will but thine be done"—and the self-forgetful way in which he sustains his mission to its final end. He ascribes all power to the Father in and through whom all things are possible. However we may answer the question of Jesus' own self-consciousness and the extent of his awareness of his mission and office, the fact remains that he constantly lived, taught and died as one "under orders." That is to say, he repeatedly acknowledged the source of his power to be in the Father who had sent him. The point is crucial because it furnishes a clue to the manner in which Jesus, though human, breaks the tragic circle of man's estrangement. The mystery of Christ consists precisely in his power to reverse in himself the self-assertive orientation; he reconciles man and God in a deed from which every trace of self-assertiveness has been removed. He gives himself in a total love to God and for man. This is precisely what no mere man in the circular predicament can do. Emphasize the humanity of Christ we must, as we must also not lose the experiential dimension of his existence as a model of true selfhood. He possesses a faith, a love and a power transcending humanity because the flaw in man is overcome through the non-self-assertive act which flows from a self with God as its center.

It is important to notice that the achievement of the one who embodies God's intention to resolve the circular predicament passes beyond a message and even beyond every idea. Christ in first loving the reconciliation of God and man in a Beloved Community is at the same time able to *establish* that community as a reality in history. Just as Christ not only preaches God's intention but also embodies it in himself, he not only preaches the reconciliation made possible in and through the Beloved Community but actually establishes that community in his own sacrificial and non-self-assertive act. In this respect the being of Christ transcends even his own speaking. For it is one thing to make a claim and quite another actually to realize that claim. One is reminded of the remark of Kant to the effect that while honesty may be the best policy, actual honesty is far higher in worth than any policy. The singularity of Christ is that he actually embodies what he proclaims to be the truth, and it is that embodiment even more than his words which exercises the authority capable of commanding assent. One sees this clearly in the conflict with the Pharisees over Jesus' authority reported in the New Testament. Jesus could come as one who "speaks with authority" because of his conviction that he actually possessed it in his own being. The irony is that the Pharisees *claimed* to have authority, but they did not actually have it. Jesus felt his authority in a mode which made it unnecessary for him to claim it for himself and, in fact, he often subordinated himself, as when, for example, he responded to the address, "Good Teacher . . ." (Luke 18:18) by saying, "Why callest thou me good? None is good save one—God" (Luke 18:19). This subordination belongs to the person who performs in the non-self-assertive mode and who accomplishes his mission by manifesting the love which overcomes the estrangement of man from God.

In establishing the Beloved Community, foreshadowed in the teaching about the Kingdom of God, Christ brought into reality a new being, a locus of transforming power where many members are called together through faith into a unity with the divine self. The natural body is sown, and there arises from Christ's sacrificial death the spiritual body which is the church. The question is, How does this new reality and the deed by which it was established give us insight into the nullification of the alienation which resulted from man's rejection of God in favor of himself? Nothing done can be undone in the literal sense of never having happened, which is to say that for faith the resolution of man's predicament does *not* take the form—as it does in some Eastern religions—of a subsequent discovery that man's predicament was not real in the first place or that it was the result of a misconception. The rejection of God is there both as a fact and as a continuing possibility, but it is now seen in a new perspective and set in relation to a new power for dealing with it. What Christ, as the embodiment of God's intention, discloses is precisely the intention to forgive man if he will repent and accept the forgiveness thus made possible even though he has no claim on that forgiveness and cannot achieve it himself. Thus one comes to look upon the rejection of God in a new light; no one caught in the circle of self-assertiveness can either expiate that rejection or transform himself by his own power. Christ can accomplish both precisely because he is, though human, more than man; what he reveals is that while man cannot be reoriented and reconciled with God of his own resources, he can come to accept the forgiveness and reconciliation of One who desires not the death but the redemption of the transgressor. The proof of this reconciliation consists in the fact that the Beloved Community uniting God and man is actually brought into existence by the sacrificial death of Christ —the concrete embodiment of the divine intention to forgive; one accepts this forgiveness itself and as a result is incorporated into a spiritual community not of saints but of sinners who believe that they are accepted and are prisoners of the hope that they can be transformed. The members of this community live in the memory that it was established not of themselves but for them by the One who first loved it and was willing to die that it might come into being.

We have an analogy in human experience of the process I have just outlined, and it is recorded for us in the well-known story of Joseph and his brothers so central for the ancient Hebraic tradition. They start with a human community of love and trust rooted in the unity of the family bond. As the inevitable result of man's tendency to compare his lot with that of others in order to see whether he is receiving the justice which he supposes is his desert, envy and hatred are born. Joseph's brothers are stirred with jealousy against him, for, after all, they argue, Joseph is but one among us and there is no reason why he should receive favors denied to us. So motivated, they turn against him in anger and abandon him; in casting him aside they break their community of love and trust. When next they meet and circumstances are entirely changed, the brothers are fearful because they expect Joseph to judge them and treat them in accordance with the same standard of justice which determined their dealings with him. And well he might have done so, were his aim simply to exact a penalty for the wrongs he suffered at their hands. But the question which surely occurred to Joseph is this: Would the exaction of a penalty in accordance with retributive justice do more than strike a balance; would it succeed in re-establishing their community, or would it not, rather, lead to new and more bitter hatred among them? Joseph, though wronged, nevertheless sacrificed his claim and forgave them. In that act, their community was reborn and was placed on a far higher and more intimate plane than before, because its previous existence was rooted in a natural family bond, but now its life springs from a sacrificial act exhibiting love in the form of forgiveness.[1]

Earlier it was said that any interpretation of faith concerning the accomplishment of Christ would have to meet two conditions. First, some event had to happen or some change had to take place in reality, and this change was to represent something more than a change in human thought or attitude; and second, the event had to have a form which allows for its appropriation by man as a creature of freedom and self-consciousness. Let me now show how what we have said about Christ as the concrete manifestation of the divine intention satisfies these conditions.

The real change required is found in the total phenomenon of Jesus as Christ, especially in his obedient sacrifice of himself and its manifestation of the divine intention to overcome the world through forgiveness. Resulting from that deed is the actual existence of the Beloved Community, a new reality which no mere man can establish. And this community, as its name implies, is sustained by the living power of the divine self. Coming into human history, therefore, is a reality which transcends both thought and language, though it requires both for its understanding and communication. It is necessary to stress this new reality because faith is not properly understood if it is supposed

1. Cf. Josiah Royce, *The Problem of Christianity* (Chicago, 1968) for a similar use of the Joseph story.

that the disclosure of the divine self in Christ leaves everything as before and merely adds a new insight, or a new interpretation. William James made a similar point in criticizing the idealist interpretation of religion for its understanding of God as an absolute knower of the world as a whole; on that view it is difficult to see how God might make a difference at particular points in experience or in specific human events. The historical character of the process of God's disclosure in Christ and the actual existence of the Beloved Community testify to specific changes in reality intended to resolve man's circular predicament. Faith and understanding, to be sure, are necessary conditions for receiving and appropriating these changes, but neither faith nor understanding as such *constitute* these changes.

Though the redeeming deed stands beyond man's consciousness and the capacity of his will, it cannot remain unrelated to that consciousness. The redeeming deed would have no significance for the life of any individual unless its meaning could be grasped and appropriated. At any time one can be confronted with the message and work of Christ mediated through the Scriptures and the continuing historical institutions which give body to the Beloved Community in time. The confrontation calls for a response and the appropriate response is faith, a centered act of the finite self. The person is to understand that Christ embodies the divine intention to accept him, though he is, as the self-assertive man, unacceptable, and that he may receive the fruits of the transforming power of God through the Beloved Community if he acknowledges his guilt and accepts Jesus as Christ in faith. At this point an experiential understanding of faith becomes essential, because the confrontation with Christ is unintelligible apart from an understanding of the circular predicament. There is little point in holding up the figure of Christ as the One who delivers from that predicament, unless the predicament is understood and acknowledged. Here the circle of faith closes; the flaw in man, which is at the same time his need, is to be overcome by the Deliverer. For any person who does not acknowledge that need, however, Christ has no significance save as an obscure figure in the world's history. It therefore belongs to the task of understanding faith to emphasize man's flaw in the most concrete forms of human experience—social, political, moral, personal—because that flaw infects *all* the relationships into which he enters. What most needs to be made clear is that when one speaks about Christ as the agent who overcomes man's flaw, one is also speaking about the fundamental cause underlying the manifold distortions, tensions, conflicts and hatreds which determine the relations between man and man. The concreteness of faith has often been obscured by failure to make clear the human experience to which theological concepts point. The result is that contemporary relevance of faith is lost. We attempt to cope with human problems through science, or engineering methods, or through psychology, or again we seek assistance from a multitude of pseudo-religious forms, all the time failing to understand that the underlying problem—the circle of self-assertiveness—is exactly the problem which faith diagnoses and proposes to resolve. The failure is one of understanding and the remoteness of traditional theological language. People come to believe that Christ presides over a realm other than the one in which we live, and that he has to do only with "religion," which many have set aside, and not with life, which no one can escape.

Thus far I have been using without special explanation the expression "Beloved Community," a term for which I am indebted to Josiah Royce. In the final chapter I hope to elucidate that expression and indicate why I believe it is a peculiarly apt one for reminding us of the togetherness of persons before God, a fact often obscured by the excessive individualism of Protestantism. I wish to close this chapter, however, by explaining briefly why I regard the community as of vital importance for the understanding of faith. Since, as I have pointed out previously, the phenomenon of Christ must be understood as a total affair embracing not only the earthly ministry, but also his sacrificial death and reappearance in the spiritual body, it follows that the meaning of Christ could only be apprehended by those first "called out" to form the church. It is therefore only within the confines of the spiritual community which Christ established that the meaning of his life and work could be understood. The task of the members of those early communities was to understand what had happened to them in their experience of being "called out" from the world in Christ's name. The key to that understanding was to be found in the meaning of the one who constituted their community. The activity and thought of St. Paul must be understood in this light. Only after the divine intention had been disclosed was it possible to attempt the task of understanding and interpretation. Those, therefore, who contrast Paul's attempts to say who Christ is and what he means, with the faith preached by Jesus in the Gospel records, miss the point. Had Christ not been interpreted from the standpoint of those who were in the only position to witness the disclosure of the divine self in completed form—the members of the Beloved Community—Jesus would have appeared as nothing more than the last of the prophets with some devoted followers. The fact is, as we now know, the record of Jesus' earthly ministry itself would never have been preserved were it not for the fact that he was accepted by those first members of the Beloved Community as the one who concretely embodied the divine intention.

VII

The Beloved Community as the Locus
of Transforming Power

Faith poses a perplexing problem for understanding when it speaks, on the one hand, of the divine self as omnipresent and inescapable even if one flees to the uttermost parts of the sea, and yet, as present in a peculiar way at particular times and places culminating in a unique historical life. The divine self as creator is present by intention in all created reality and in this sense is related to the entire creation. The divine self as sustainer is present by intention in the historical order as well, related to all moments and epochs in human history. Both nature and history as such manifest omnipresence. And yet faith envisages special times and special spaces marked off from all other times and places because of their capacity to manifest the divine presence in some peculiar way. We do not think of Christ as merely one person among others, nor do we think of the Beloved Community as merely one community among others. In both cases some special mode of presence of the divine self is believed to be realized.

How can this be? Is it intelligible to say that a reality can be both uniformly present throughout the entire creation and "more" present at some points than at others? Prima facie, it would seem that this is impossible and therefore that we do not correctly express what is meant when we think in quantitative terms. Common sense regards a reality as either present or not present and it attaches no meaning to the proposition that any reality is more or less present. And yet this is not entirely true, as can been seen from consideration of a number of ordinary experiences. We do speak of a person being more or less completely engaged in a project or of one person giving more of himself than another in some cooperative endeavor. And, even more pointedly, we speak of a person revealing his character more fully at some times than at others. These quantitative expressions seem to admit of degree and thus to qualify the belief that there is a total disjunction between presence and absence. Nevertheless, there are reasons why it is not adequate to deal with the problem posed by the concepts of omnipresence and special presence in terms of a merely quantitative difference. In the first place, the Western Roman Catholic church was right in resisting the attempts of the Greek tradition to incorporate Christ into a sacred hierarchy based on degrees of being, of truth and of good. Christ, the Latin church insisted, should not be regarded as a particular degree in a scale, but only as the full embodiment of God not to be understood in terms of more and less or of continuous approximations. For faith, the divine self is expressed in Christ, and the expression transcends the distinction of more and less. To explain this transcendence one must say that whereas the divine self was *present to* a Moses, an Isaiah, or a Paul, it was not *present in* any one of them in the sense of the full presence in Christ.

Second, there is a meaning expressed in the distinction between omnipresence and special presence which completely eludes quantitative understanding. When we speak of special events in the biblical record as revelatory of the transcending center[1] we mean that these events have peculiar significance; they take place like all events at a specific time, but they are meant to manifest the divine intention for *all* times, and therefore they are set apart from ordinary historical moments. These events appear in the perspective of faith as somehow making clear the ultimate meaning of human existence. The pattern or some feature of the

1. The distinction is between *any time* and this *special* or *right time*, the latter being designated in the New Testament by the term καιρος in contrast with χρονος, which means the uniform time of a clock. Jesus is said to come εν καιρω, which means a special time of fulfillment marked off from every other time. See "Time, Times and the 'Right Time'; *Chronos* and *Kairos,*" *The Monist,* Vol. 53, No. 1 (Jan. 1969), pp. 1-13.

pattern underlying the entire historical process—*all times*—is made clear to us at these special times because in them the will of the divine self is transparently present. Omnipresence can be understood through the belief that all times and spaces are related to the divine intention whereas not every occasion discloses the meaning of existence as a whole.

The Beloved Community is a special locus of the divine presence in the form of the Spirit unifying many diverse selves. Though extended over space taken geographically, this community exists primarily in time as the continuing witness to God's intention in history. Though similar in structure to other communities, the Beloved Community is not to be regarded as merely one among many. For it is in its ideal dimension a sacred locus of transforming power, made up of members gathered or called together in Christ's name and unified by the animating spirit of love. As the special locus of the divine self it has the mission of being the redemptive community. Other human communities are concerned with some partial or limited character of life—educational, professional, political, social, etc.—but the Beloved Community is concerned with man's being and with the orientation of life as a whole. This community has the means of overcoming man's self-assertiveness because it was founded by a sacrificial or non-self-assertive act. The Beloved Community was born through a form of love which remains alive within it as the bond uniting the members. Previously Christ was described as the concrete embodiment of the divine intention to resolve the circular predicament; now the Beloved Community appears as the means whereby that intention is to be realized through history.

Let us consider the nature of a community and why it is important to use this term in place of the more familiar term "church." The English term "church" has not retained the connotation of εκκλησια, or "those called out" in faith, and it has the further disadvantage of having become identified exclusively with an institution and its structure. A community, however, is not identical with an institution or organizational structure and still less with a physical habitation. The Roman Catholic tradition tended to understand the church in terms of the doctrine of Incarnation.

The church was regarded as an extension in time of Christ's embodiment; the result was that the church came to be identified primarily as an institution structured in accordance with a hierarchy of offices and a well-defined line of authority for discharging all the functions of the ecclesiastical organization. This understanding of the church is not without its truth, and who knows better than the many branches of Protestantism how difficult it is to structure the church for effective work in the world and retain the continuity of faith at the same time. Nevertheless, there has been in the traditional Catholic doctrine with its stress on the Second Person, a curious neglect of the Third Person, a neglect of the Spirit which lives, animates and transforms. The historical reasons for this fact need not concern us; the capacity of the divine spirit to break, transform and restructure old forms and offices must inevitably cause anxiety for those upholding law and order. The fact is that the Spirit is under no obligation to appear as the obedient consecrator of the organizations made by man. On the contrary, through an individual or a group the Spirit may come as the prophetic judge of these organizations, exposing their failure at just the point where they mistake ecclesiastical organization and authority for the living unity of faith and love between persons. The essential office of the Spirit is to create community—a spiritual bond between the members—and it is by no means obvious that some particular form of ecclesiastical polity represents the only one through which the Beloved Community is to be organized. The problem of ecclesiastical polity has frequently been exaggerated; more important is the rediscovery of the concept of the church as a community, a spiritual linkage between otherwise distinguishable individuals which depends more on their faith and love than on any political form which it may assume in the historical order.

We may now return to the question as to the nature of a community, and the special character of the Beloved Community. To begin with, a community, though a togetherness of distinct individuals, is not to be confused with a crowd, a mob, or a collection of people who *happen* to be together because of some event—a concert, a play, an athletic contest—which attracts their attention. These collections do not constitute communities because they are largely transient in character; they may be re-formed continually, as in the case of the crowd which returns each week to witness a sporting event, or they may appear in uninterrupted form, as in the case of the shoppers who are always in the shops. In both cases we have many people doing or witnessing the same thing, but they do not on this account form a community; what brings them together is not itself sufficiently time-spanning or significant to weld them into a unity overcoming their separateness. A community, on the other hand, has an identity which enables us to understand it as an individual reality enduring through time and having a life of its own. Two factors ultimately determine the identity and the life-span of any community; the universality and enduring significance of the purpose which defines it, and the urgency of the need which it fulfills or overcomes in the life of the individual who joins it. The fundamental fact about a community is that it is both a form and a power unifying many distinct selves; in classical philosophical language, a community is a unity of a *one* and a *many*. In setting forth the nature of community, it is necessary to view it from two sides: first, from the side of the unity or the community in its own life, and second, from the side of the many, or the individual members who belong to it. Starting with the community itself the question is: What constitutes it as a unity? For an answer we must discover what it is that has the power to unify many selves and to sustain that unity in a living way so that we pass beyond abstract unity and reach a constant *unifying* power which is the form of life itself. The ground of this unifying is the purpose or goal for which the community exists. The goal is what attracts the members, selects them from others and calls forth their dedication as those who are brought together because of it. When each member explicitly acknowledges that goal as either *a* purpose in his life or, in the case of the Beloved Community, as *the* overarching purpose of his existence, we have a situation in which the many, though distinct as individuals, are yet unified. For present in the life of each member is the *same* animating power of the purpose which all acknowledge.

If the community is to extend through time and have a historical life of its own it must exhibit in its own structure the modes of time, which is to say that at any *present* moment in the life of the community the members must be capable of *remembering* its *past*—especially the event or events which brought it into being —and of *anticipating* the hoped-for *future* which would be the concrete realization of that hope. When we speak of a community as a spiritual togetherness we are pointing to the fact that its life quite literally mirrors the pattern of self-conscious and intentional life which each of us verifies in his own experience of memory and anticipation. Let us consider more closely how the past and future of the community enter into its life. These modes of time make their appearance through various forms of *celebration*[2] in which the members are reminded both of the past from which they spring and of the purpose or goal which unifies their life and sustains the life of their community. The celebration of the past is aimed at making vivid in the present the meaning of the founder of the community and the purpose on which it was founded. This celebration is a reminder that the past belongs to and forms a living part of the life of each member. Similarly with regard to the hoped-for future. The goal of the community is held before the members in imagination and vision as that concrete realization for which they strive and which is to be effected in and through them. Each member sees the goal as belonging to, and in the case of the religious community as defining the purpose of, his life. The founder and his goal, therefore, provide both as a remembered ideal in principle and as an anticipated realization in fact the unifying power which continually transforms the distinct and otherwise separated many into the unity of life and experience which is their community.

The purpose of the community comes to the members both in idea and in power. It is in idea insofar as the members must understand the purpose to which they are dedicated. But the

2. Celebration is a fundamental concept in the philosophy of religion because it is the foundation of liturgy. I have indicated some of its features in "The Experience of the Holy and the Idea of God," in J. M. Edie, ed., *Phenomenology in America* (Chicago, 1967), pp. 295-306.

purpose is more than an idea to be apprehended or thought; it lives as well as an animating force motivating the behavior of those who claim devotion to it. It is not enough to say that the members possess the purpose and have control over it; it is more accurate to say that the purpose possesses them insofar as they have given themselves over to it as the determining power either of their lives as a whole or of some particular facet of their existence. Moreover, in a nominalistic and highly individualistic age such as the present, it is imperative to make clear that the purpose which unifies a community transcends all the members individually. As Royce pointed out years ago, we shall never understand community if we view it in nominalistic fashion, starting with one member and then another and another, as if we were dealing with a collection to be added up. A community is more than individual members together, even together in one place and time, for as we have seen, a crowd or a mob fulfills that condition; moreover it makes no sense to speak of "members" unless there is some identifiable unifying force which defines the enduring community to which they belong. We can, to be sure, count the members once they are identified and in that sense there is a sum, but there is no other sense in which it is intelligible to speak of a sum. The purpose, the devotion and loyalty which unify the community cannot be regarded as the sum of anything. What binds the members is a literally spiritual bond between them which, though present in each, transcends them all, and this is the reason communities continue to exist when their members are not physically present to each other. It is the refusal of the modern nominalistic consciousness to admit the reality of such spiritual bonds which leads it to approach the problem of community either by viewing the individuals one at a time, or by supposing that *somehow* adding or compounding them will elicit the desired unity. But viewing individuals one at a time does not bring us into the presence of a community; on the contrary, we are left with just so many individuals. Compounding them in some way may lead to a collectivity, but again, not to a community. There is no way of understanding a community without introducing unifying elements which are not the exclusive possession of any single individual, because they transcend all the members and serve to define the reality to which they, as members, belong. This point holds true for all communities, secular or sacred, but it has special significance for the understanding of faith concerning the Beloved Community.

Thus far we have viewed the community from the side of the one or of the community as an identifiable unity. Before considering what is distinctive of the Beloved Community, we must direct attention to the side of the many, the side of the members themselves. To *be* a member of any community one must *become* a member, which means a free acknowledgment that one stands in need of the unity of loyalty and devotion which that community provides. This acknowledgment is a purposive and self-determined act on the part of the would-be member, distinguishing him from the indiscriminate individual who is not serious and who comes to be known in the popular mind as a "joiner." In addition to acknowledging the need for that community the individual must also be willing to accept as part of himself the purpose for which the community exists. That is to say, depending on the specific nature of the community in question, the individual must identify himself, either in part or totally, with the purpose or goal defining the community he professes to join. In fact this means that a member identifies himself with a self which has been extended to include within itself the common past of the community and the future toward which it moves. For each person, becoming a member means coming to accept as "mine" the memory and hope of the community. Earlier in our discussion, we saw that the self is not an object to be sensed nor a substance that mysteriously underlies all that we think and do, but a center of intention and a time-spanning purpose unifying our entire existence. This conception of the self is well adapted for furnishing insight into what takes place when an individual person joins or is incorporated into a community. No one has total control over the contents that go to make up his career in time as the individual self which he is. I may seek to dissociate myself from a past deed or no longer continue to accept a past belief, but I cannot by an act of will alone banish these contents from myself, nor have I much control of the many adventitious events that constitute my history. On the other hand, we clearly have some control over our own identity, since we can decide to become engaged in, or to reject, causes or communities which seek our allegiance. When we engage ourselves or seek to be incorporated into a community, we at the same time accept certain extensions of ourselves: we identify ourselves with the common past and the common future of that community and accept both as part of our individual history. Loyal acceptance of membership marks the transition from "I" to "we." We no longer view that past and future from the standpoint of spectator because it now belongs essentially to our own lives. Thus Abraham Lincoln, speaking to and for the nation as a community, does *not* say "the forefathers brought forth . . ." or "some forefathers . . ." but "*our* forefathers . . . ," and in speaking in the first person plural, he utters what every member would and should say himself as a member of the community whose past is being rehearsed.

In addition to acknowledging his need of the community and to accepting its purpose in loyalty and devotion, the would-be member also commits himself to a line of conduct which contributes to the realization of the purpose for which the community exists. Here the active and practical dimension of community comes into view. If communities aim to achieve results and to transform the shape of things, they must elicit from their members something more than a *profession* of loyalty and devotion. The intention to become a living member must find its fulfillment in a course of life which fosters the community's aim and contribute to individual self-realization at the same time. Community is more than a bond of understanding and cooperation between its members; it is also a locus of transforming power making itself felt in the lives of its members and in the course of the complex affairs of the epoch in which it exists. In short, in virtue of its peculiar structure as a living unity of a one and a many, a community is ideally fitted for performing the double-barreled task of reorienting its members and providing them with a purpose which constitutes them as persons, and of transforming the social, political and cultural world in which both the members and their community exist.

The foregoing account of community is based on experience of human cooperative enterprises and on an analysis of the structure exhibited by them. This experience, following our pattern of finding an experiential understanding of faith, must now serve as an analogue helping us to grasp the meaning which faith attaches to the church or Beloved Community. That community shares the structure to be found in any community however limited or partial its purpose may be; it also differs from all other communities in a crucial way. The Beloved Community is the redeeming community, which means that its purpose transcends partial and limited concerns and reaches to the intentional center of the selves who are its members. The purpose of that community defines the overarching purpose, which, as we saw, constitutes individual selfhood.

Let us begin, as before, and consider the Beloved Community from the side of its unity and identity in time. The Beloved Community is the spiritual body with Christ as its head; it finds concrete realization as the unity of the many wherever "two or three are gathered together" in his name. The ground of that unity is the *agape* or charity of the divine self made manifest in Christ's being and in his sacrificial deed. That special form of other-regarding love, about which Paul wrote so eloquently in his Epistle to the Church at Corinth, constitutes the principal spiritual link which binds the many members into one living whole. *Agape* manifests itself in a multitude of forms and relations. There is the love which the divine self has for the members, and the love which the members have for the divine self; there is the reciprocal love of the members for each other based on their common knowledge that each is the object of the divine love; and finally there is the love which the members have for the Beloved Community itself in the form of their acceptance in faith of the forgiveness which it signalizes, and their devotion to the purpose for which it exists—the preaching of the Christian message and the extension of the divine *agape* or forgiveness among men. The third relationship is sometimes overlooked because of our failure to understand that the Beloved Community is a real being, the concrete means whereby the divine intention to resolve the human predicament is to be realized through the historical order. The Beloved Community, therefore, has a mission in history; it is the locus of transforming power breaking the tragic circle of self-assertiveness and reorienting men through faith and love to God as the ground and goal of their existence. The constancy of this mission as the expression of the divine intention, and as the object of faith and devotion for the individual members, constitutes the identity of the community through time.

The Beloved Community has its sacred past to be recollected in the memory of its members, and it has likewise its sacred future apprehended by its members in hope. Though the crucial event of the sacred past for the Beloved Community is its founding in the death of Christ, its past reaches farther back in time to the foreshadowing events of Old Testament history. The disclosure there of the divine self as the Father who calls forth the people of God constitutes a record which belongs to the past of the community established by Christ. Therefore, those abortive attempts made from time to time within the Christian churches to cut the Old Testament adrift, so to speak, and be done with the events, the ritual and the confusing lore of Hebraic history, must always be rejected. To understand the purpose and mission of the Beloved Community in history it is necessary to understand the indispensability of its total past stemming from Old Testament religion. The founding of that community represents the end of a quest which is identical with the quest for the Deliverer; if we are deprived of the full record of that quest, the meaning of its fulfillment is much diminished.

In addition to the divine disclosure in the Old Testament, the sacred past includes as well the total phenomenon of Christ and the history of man's attempts to provide an organizational body for the Beloved Community in the earthly city. Nor should we overlook the tragic chapters of this history, chapters during which the Beloved Community had to exist in the face of schism and division between the historical churches, chapters so filled with strife and hatred that no one in possession of his senses could say, as was reported to have been said in Roman times, "How these Christians love each other." What such tragic interludes teach, however, is that the spirit of love which ultimately unifies and sustains the Beloved Community is not a static and unchanging unity, fixed once for all above the temporal world, but instead a dynamic life which aims to overcome strife and to reconcile those at war with each other. For just as that community itself was born in a triumph of love and reconciliation over the separation of death, so in its history that same community finds its life in overcoming alienation. Every deed of reconciliation is at the same time an extension of the purpose for which the community exists.

The Beloved Community has not only its sacred past, which forms an identical part of the past of every member, but also its sacred future apprehended in hope. A full account of that hope would take us far beyond present purposes. The chief consideration is to understand the anticipated future in its function as a unifying element both for the community itself and for its members. Insofar as the community has a mission which is not yet accomplished, it has both a life and a future. The hoped-for presentation of the Christian message to all who listen and the extension of the transforming power found in the divine forgiveness represent proximate goals. Every would-be member of the community must commit himself to those goals so that they form a part of his own future, and his own hope. A powerful source of unification among the many members is found in the fact that the anticipated future of the community is at the same time the envisaged future of every member. Each one, that is to say, knows that every other member, as one who maintains the bond of loyalty, is convicted by the same ultimate hope to which he himself is committed. Thus a multitude of distinct individuals, vastly separated by time and space, are nevertheless joined together in a bond of understanding, a power exercised by the common hope they each acknowledge.

Let us turn now to the individuals, the side of the many, and see how they are to become related to and brought within the life of the Beloved Community. To begin with, the community is there as a reality already founded, and as such it stands beyond the consciousness of any member to whom it offers the forgiveness of God. The first step to be taken by an individual vis-à-vis this community is an acknowledgment of the flaw in himself, an acknowledgment of the self-assertive basis of his existence in the circular predicament, an acknowledgment of his need for the transforming power which lives in and through the members. The community, to be sure, needs him if its purpose is to be achieved, but at the outset his need for the community is far more important. The man in the circular predicament is unable from his own resources to break out of the circle of self-assertiveness. But he may become related to a source of power which accomplishes what he cannot; this power is to be found in the Beloved Community precisely because it was established by a deed which broke through the tragic circle of self-assertion. The individual's acknowledgment of his need for the community is at the same time his confession that he leads a self-centered rather than a God-centered existence. The next step is acceptance of the divine forgiveness which Christ discloses as the divine intention, and this acceptance is faith. Faith is here the title deed to membership in the Beloved Community; it is faith in the transforming love of God manifested in Christ and sustained in his Community; it is faith in the divine promise of self-fulfillment which can come only through commitment to the love of God and of the neighbor.

Being incorporated into the life of the Beloved Community means the acceptance of a new overarching purpose defining and determining the center of the self. When one accepts the founder and the purpose of his community, he has the love of God and of his neighbors as the center of his intention. It is in this sense that we can speak of a new self or new nature coming into being: "I live, yet not I, but Christ liveth in me." And the mode of this indwelling is the animating force of a new overarching purpose. And as one lives within the transforming power of love and devotion which pervades the community, one has resources for the continual overcoming of all the forces, both in himself and in the world, which lead him back to the self-assertive form of existence. The term "continual" is of special importance because it points to the dynamic element at the heart of the Beloved Community. The set of spiritual bonds unifying the many members is not a safe enclosure, a timeless and unchanging refuge whereby one escapes the problems of the world. On the contrary, it is a source of power within the historical order which makes possible the continual overcoming of the world through the members who live in it and in the world at the same time. According to faith, God was in Christ reconciling the world unto himself; from the perspective of the Beloved Community this means that Christ is in the world carrying on this process. And insofar as any member lives and acts in the world, taking part with others in many enterprises reaching beyond the confines of the Beloved Community, the influence of Christian love is felt in that world both individually and socially.

It is now possible to make clear the dual nature of the Beloved Community. It is a special locus of transforming power because it is the unique habitat of the Spirit; as was pointed out previously, the community is the special presence of the divine self as love which supplements the omnipresence or total relatedness of God to the entire creation. Though a special sacred locus, however, the Beloved Community and its individual members both exist in the secular world. The ancient problem, therefore, of the relation between sacred and secular cannot be avoided. This is a perennial problem for the history and philosophy of religion, but it has special importance at present because of the radical secularization taking place in the modern world. In considering now the relations between the Beloved Community and the secular order in which it exists, the discussion has come full circle; it began with the fact of secularization as one of the chief reasons why it is necessary to find a fresh approach to the continuing enterprise of faith seeking understanding, and it returns to the fact in the discovery that the Beloved Community exists in the secular world.

Despite the negative connotation that attaches to the term "secularism" as meaning the denial of the sacred and the attempt to found human life on a wholly naturalistic basis, it is important to remember that biblical religion does not regard the world as inherently evil or as a mere passing show which has no substantial existence. The fact is that the Judeo-Christian tradition, in contradistinction to some other religions, accepts, and even insists upon, the reality of nature, history, and individual human existence. Moreover, in the light of faith, man is given dominion over the world, and in exercising his mandate he creates a world of secular culture. The development of civilization in the West clearly illustrates the process; the influence of the Judeo-Christian tradition in that development helps in part to explain why an autonomous, technological culture could emerge in the West as over against those civilizations whose dominant religions denied full reality to the world and to history, retreating from it to a wholly spiritual sphere which leaves the world and the historical process unaffected. Therefore, when faith confronts the secular world it does so in full awareness of that world as the development through man's freedom of the potentialities inherent in creation. The "world" may have its temptations and its own seductive power distracting man from divine things, but from the standpoint of faith the world is not to be set aside as evil. In the end, the redemptive community saves man through the world and not by removing him from it. Therefore, as I shall propose, the sacred in the form of the Beloved Community must be related in some intimate and fruitful way to the secular order, and the relation will have to be a dialectical one because the two orders overlap.

From a logical point of view, three archetypal relations may obtain between the two orders. Since we deal here with archetypes we must understand that they represent limiting cases never to be found fully exemplified in any historical situations. First, the sacred and the secular may exist in complete disjunction or as entirely separate, existing side by side and without essential interaction. On this alternative the Beloved Community would exist encapsulated within itself and set over against the world. Second, the attempt may be made to reduce one to the other, starting from either side. If a start is made with the secular, the Beloved Community is deprived of its special significance as the intensive locus of transforming power and its transcendent source is denied. Human existence is then regarded as entirely "mundane," the world and the secular city become a final habitation, and the city which is out of sight is forgotten. Man then envisages no limit or law for his existence beyond the one which he gives to himself. Self-assertive existence meets no challenge and man is left to resolve his circular predicament entirely from his own resources. Secular life would, so to speak, cover the whole ground, and the death of God would exhaust the secular litany.

If a start were made from the side of the sacred, the Beloved Community and its life would be seen as encompassing and constituting the whole of existence. The secular would disappear as such, swallowed up entirely by sacred life. The historical model for this alternative in Western civilization is found in the theocratic ideal where life and power are so structured that control resides completely in the sacred order. Each moment of life equally bears the whole weight of eternity and all of human existence is spiritualized and becomes transparently divine. A similar motive is at work in all forms of monasticism, both East and West. The attempt is to construct a special and wholly sacred space and time within which the religious life can be lived and its precepts carried out in every detail. Although it is true that monastic orders have generally existed in the midst of secular cultures (a fact which might lead us to take them as representative of the disjunctive relation between sacred and secular), the monastic form itself illustrates the total sacred in the sense that it is meant to exhaust life. There is but one life and it is entirely sacred.

The third alternative involves, on the one hand, an acknowledgment of the distinction between the two orders and, on the other, the recognition of a fruitful interaction between them which takes the form of a creative tension involving mutual criticism. It is this alternative which faith envisages and demands. Neither of the other alternatives is acceptable. In the first place, the Beloved Community does not and cannot exist in a disjunctive relation to the world and secular culture, unaffected by either and having no influence on the course of human history. For this solution means abandoning the world to the powers, including the demonic powers, and thus runs counter to the divine intention to transform the world. The second alternative in either of its forms is not more acceptable by faith insofar as we are speaking from the perspective of human history. For it is obvious that faith cannot accept the reduction of the Beloved Community to a wholly secular status, nor can it admit that a naturalistic foundation for life is sufficient. On the other hand, faith acknowledges the reality of the secular order as the sphere of proximate or limited concerns and as the result of man's creative activity in knowing the world, seeking to overcome the evils in it, and in developing its latent possibilities. Therefore, the secular order is not devoured by the sacred nor held captive within its limits. There is much in the worlds of science and of art, of technology and of scholarship, that has not been developed under religious auspices and is not the unique product of any sacred order. Of the three possible relationships between sacred and secular, only the third remains; the two are dialectically related in a way that precludes both their disjunction and their reduction one to the other.

If the two orders are recognized as distinct but not separated from each other, then they must interact with each other in various ways. The existence of the Beloved Community must make a difference to the secular world and the fact that it exists in that world must make a difference to the Beloved Community. Naturally, an extended account of those interactions falls beyond our scope. There is, however, one mode of the relationship which is of vital importance at present. Following the biblical model of the prophetic word expressing criticism and judgment, let us consider in what way the Beloved Community expresses this judgment on the modern secular world, and conversely how the secular world is made to function as a prophetic critic of the Beloved Community at least insofar as it is embodied in actual institutions. The judgment from the side of the Beloved Community takes the form of a reminder and a warning that secular existence left to itself and unmindful of limits set by the divine self leads inevitably to the absolutizing of man, his powers and perspectives. The main result is an extending and deepening of the circular predicament. But there is a judgment proceeding in the opposite direction, and it is one which Reformed Christianity well knows in terms of the experience of its founders. All finite realities, including the church itself, are subject to divine judgment in virtue of the fact that they are open to corruption. Churches have been inclined to forget that, though they express the word of judgment in accordance with the divine intention, they are not free of the need to be judged themselves. Those to whom the prophet Amos preached overlooked this truth when they supposed that the Day of Jahweh would be one of light and not darkness. But as it turned out the people most known of God were most severely judged. So it is with the church. It must accomplish the most difficult task set for man; it must keep alive within itself a principle or a channel of self-judgment. The reason this task is so difficult stems from the chief temptation faced by the church: to base its authority among men on the belief that it is beyond all criticism. The strength of this temptation is so great that we cannot expect the church, administered as it is by fallible men, to resist it wholly from *within;* the prophetic voice from *without* is therefore necessary. My proposal is that the spirit leading into all truth uses the voice of secular society as a means of keeping the institutional forms which embody the Beloved Community from being absolutized so that they either obscure God or tyrannize men. The Assyrians, Babylonians, Persians and Greeks in biblical perspective were raised up as instruments of chastisement; why may not the secular city exercise a similar function? In the one direction the prophetic voice of the Beloved Community draws the boundaries that keep man from absolutizing himself; in the other direction the prophetic voice comes through the secular society reminding the churches that they too stand under judgment and that they too are capable of absolutizing themselves. There is thus a dynamic tension between the two orders and mutual criticism exercised by one on the other.

Let us conclude by looking more closely at the interaction between the two at a focal point—the claim to autonomy which has signalized the emergence of modern secular society since the period of Enlightenment. In another place[3] I have tried to define the characteristics of secularization, of which autonomy is but one. I choose it here for analysis not because it exhausts the topic but because it underlies all the others; the same analysis could be given for other features of secularization.

The principle of autonomy which received classic formulation in the thought of Kant means that each reality, but especially man, should be treated in accordance with its own proper nature. Autonomy does *not* mean being a law to oneself, as has sometimes been supposed. It means instead that respect for the nature of a person or a living creature is exacted from every other creature. Hence, as a being of reason and freedom, I am not to be treated as if I were a star or a stone, an automaton or a puppet. This principle holds regardless of the source of the depersonalizing necessity, including even the divine self. From the side of secularism this principle is also valid; the religious institution is as much bound by it as any other. This means that the Beloved Community in proposing the religious truth for acceptance must do so in full acknowledgment that the one to whom it speaks is a being of freedom and reason. Authoritarianism, or the ecclesiastical form of fascism, cannot be countenanced; if the truth cannot make its way in being preached to man, it will not fare better being imposed upon a being who has been reduced to less than man. Autonomy, then, is the prophetic and critical word of the secular order against the excesses and abuses of the Beloved Community as an institution. It is the critical principle which keeps the church from absolutizing itself.

But there is still one more side to the picture. Autonomy is a critical or limiting concept which is abstract in that it enables us to expose heteronomy but does not of itself give specific guidance for the exercise of our freedom. Autonomy, in short, needs a principle of limitation, and if it does not find one, the result is absolutization in the secular direction. Man sees himself as subject to no limit but that which he imposes on himself, but the

3. *Experience and God* (New York, 1968), Epilogue.

difficulty is that it is impossible to determine what specific norm he should impose from the formal principle of autonomy alone. Therefore, the ethical and religious guidance of the Beloved Community is needed if man is not to destroy himself, because he will not acknowledge a limit to his will. On that note we close the circle of our entire discussion which begins with the flaw in man and ends with the community—the Spiritual Body—which overcomes that flaw through the only power that ever heals anything, the power of the love that knows how to suffer in order to overcome the world.

73 74 75 10 9 8 7 6 5 4 3 2 1